LOVE & WAR
ART & GOD

LOVE & WAR
ART & GOD

The Poems of Karl Shapiro

STUART WRIGHT, *Publisher*

Library of Congress Catalog Card Number: 84–050976
ISBN 0–913773–08–5   *Paper Issue*
ISBN 0–913773–09–3   *Cloth Issue*
ISBN 0–913773–10–7   *Limited Issue*

First Edition

To Sophie

Roses in late November
Here where the skies begin
Bring poetry back to love.
Thank you for bringing them in.

Contents

LOVE

WAR

ART

GOD

LOVE

A Cut Flower

I stand on slenderness all fresh and fair,
I feel root-firmness in the earth far down,
I catch in the wind and loose my scent for bees
That sack my throat for kisses and suck love.
What is the wind that brings thy body over?
Wind, I am beautiful and sick. I long
For rain that strikes and bites like cold and hurts.
Be angry, rain, for dew is kind to me
When I am cool from sleep and take my bath.

Who softens the sweet earth about my feet,
Touches my face so often and brings water?
Where does she go, taller than any sunflower
Over the grass like birds? Has she a root?
These are great animals that kneel to us,
Sent by the sun perhaps to help us grow.
I have seen death. The colors went away,
The petals grasped at nothing and curled tight.
Then the whole head fell off and left the sky.

She tended me and held me by my stalk.
Yesterday I was well, and then the gleam,
The thing sharper than frost cut me in half.
I fainted and was lifted high. I feel
Waist-deep in rain. My face is dry and drawn.
My beauty leaks into the glass like rain.
When first I opened to the sun I thought
My colors would be parched. Where are my bees?
Must I die now? Is this a part of life?

Adam and Eve

I The Sickness of Adam

In the beginning, at every step, he turned
As if by instinct to the East to praise
The nature of things. Now every path was learned
He lost the lifted, almost flower-like gaze

Of a temple dancer. He began to walk
Slowly, like one accustomed to be alone.
He found himself lost in the field of talk;
Thinking became a garden of its own.

In it were new things: words he had never said,
Beasts he had never seen and knew were not
In the true garden, terrors, and tears shed
Under a tree by him, for some new thought.

And the first anger. Once he flung a staff
At softly coupling sheep and struck the ram.
It broke away. And God heard Adam laugh
And for his laughter made the creature lame.

And wanderlust. He stood upon the Wall
To search the unfinished countries lying wide
And waste, where not a living thing could crawl,
And yet he would descend, as if to hide.

His thought drew down the guardian at the gate,
To whom man said, "What danger am I in?"
And the angel, hurt in spirit, seemed to hate
The wingless thing that worried after sin,

For it said nothing but marvelously unfurled
Its wings and arched them shimmering overhead,
Which must have been the signal from the world
That the first season of our life was dead.

Adam fell down with labor in his bones,
And God approached him in the cool of day
And said, "This sickness in your skeleton
Is longing. I will remove it from your clay."

He said also, "I made you strike the sheep."
It began to rain and God sat down beside
The sinking man. When he was fast asleep
He wet his right hand deep in Adam's side

And drew the graceful rib out of his breast.
Far off, the latent streams began to flow
And birds flew out of Paradise to nest
On earth. Sadly the angel watched them go.

II   The Recognition of Eve

Whatever it was she had so fiercely fought
Had fled back to the sky, but still she lay
With arms outspread, awaiting its assault,
Staring up through the branches of the tree,
The fig tree. Then she drew a shuddering breath
And turned her head instinctively his way.
She had fought birth as dying men fight death.

Her sigh awakened him. He turned and saw
A body swollen, as though formed of fruits,
White as the flesh of fishes, soft and raw.
He hoped she was another of the brutes
So he crawled over and looked into her eyes,
The human wells that pool all absolutes.
It was like looking into double skies.

And when she spoke the first word (it was *thou*)
He was terror-stricken, but she raised her hand
And touched his wound where it was fading now,
For he must feel the place to understand.
Then he recalled the longing that had torn

His side, and while he watched it whitely mend,
He felt it stab him suddenly like a thorn.

He thought the woman had hurt him. Was it she
Or the same sickness seeking to return;
Or was there any difference, the pain set free
And she who seized him now as hard as iron?
Her fingers bit his body. She looked old
And involuted, like the newly-born.
He let her hurt him till she loosed her hold.

Then she forgot him and she wearily stood
And went in search of water through the grove.
Adam could see her wandering through the wood,
Studying her footsteps as her body wove
In light and out of light. She found a pool
And there he followed shyly to observe.
She was already turning beautiful.

III The Kiss

The first kiss was with stumbling fingertips.
Their bodies grazed each other as if by chance
And touched and untouched in a kind of dance.
Second, they found out touching with their lips.

Some obscure angel, pausing on his course,
Shed such a brightness on the face of Eve
That Adam in grief was ready to believe
He had lost her love. The third kiss was by force.

Their lips formed foreign, unimagined oaths
When speaking of the Tree of Guilt. So wide
Their mouths, they drank each other from inside.
A gland of honey burst within their throats.

But something rustling hideously overhead,
They jumped up from the fourth caress and hid.

IV   The Tree of Guilt

Why, on her way to the oracle of Love,
Did she not even glance up at the Tree
Of Life, that giant with whitish cast
And glinting leaves and berries of dull gray,
As though covered with mold? But who would taste
The medicine of immortality,
And who would "be as God?" And in what way?

So she came breathless to the lowlier one
And like a priestess of the cult she knelt,
Holding her breasts in token for a sign,
And prayed the spirit of the burdened bough
That the great power of the tree be seen
And lift itself out of the Tree of Guilt
Where it had hidden in the leaves till now.

Or did she know already? Had the peacock
Rattling its quills, glancing its thousand eyes
At her, the iridescence of the dove,
Stench of the he-goat, everything that joins
Told her the mystery? It was not enough,
So from the tree the snake began to rise
And dropt its head and pointed at her loins.

She fell and hid her face and still she saw
The spirit of the tree emerge and slip
Into the open sky until it stood
Straight as a standing-stone, and spilled its seed.
And all the seed were serpents of the good.
Again the snake was seized and from its lip
It spat the venomous evil of the deed.

And it was over. But the woman lay
Stricken with what she knew, ripe in her thought
Like a fresh apple fallen from the limb
And rotten, like a fruit that lies too long.
This way she rose, ripe-rotten in her prime

And spurned the cold thing coiled against her foot
And called her husband, in a kind of song.

V   The Confession

As on the first day her first word was *thou*.
He waited while she said, "Thou art the tree."
And while she said, almost accusingly,
Looking at nothing, "Thou are the fruit I took."
She seemed smaller by inches as she spoke,
And Adam wondering touched her hair and shook,
Half understanding. He answered softly, "How?"

And for the third time, in the third way, Eve:
"The tree that rises from the middle part
Of the garden." And almost tenderly, "Thou art
The garden. *We*." Then she was overcome,
And Adam coldly, lest he should succumb
To pity, standing at the edge of doom,
Comforted her like one about to leave.

She sensed departure and she stood aside
Smiling and bitter. But he asked again,
"How did you eat? With what thing did you sin?"
And Eve with body slackened and uncouth,
"Under the tree I took the fruit of truth
From an angel. I ate it with my other mouth."
And saying so, she did not know she lied.

It was the man who suddenly released
From doubt, wept in the woman's heavy arms,
Those double serpents, subtly winding forms
That climb and drop about the manly boughs,
And dry with weeping, fiery and aroused,
Fell on her face to slake his terrible thirst
And bore her body earthward like a beast.

VI Shame

The hard blood falls back in the manly fount,
The soft door closes under Venus' mount,
The ovoid moon moves to the Garden's side
And dawn comes, but the lovers have not died.
They have not died but they have fallen apart.
In sleep, like equal halves of the same heart.

How to teach shame? How to teach nakedness
To the already naked? How to express
Nudity? How to open innocent eyes
And separate the innocent from the wise?
And how to re-establish the guilty tree
In infinite gardens of humanity?

By marring the image, by the black device
Of the goat-god, by the clown of Paradise,
By fruits of cloth and by the navel's bud,
By itching tendrils and by strings of blood,
By ugliness, by the shadow of our fear,
By ridicule, by the fig-leaf patch of hair.

Whiter than tombs, whiter than whitest clay,
Exposed beneath the whitening eye of day,
They awoke and saw the covering that reveals.
They thought they were changing into animals.
Like animals they bellowed terrible cries
And clutched each other, hiding each other's eyes.

VII Exile

The one who gave the warning with his wings,
Still doubting them, held out the sword of flame
Against the Tree of Whiteness as they came
Angrily, slowly by, like exiled kings,

9

And watched them at the broken-open gate
Stare in the distance long and overlong,
And then, like peasants, pitiful and strong,
Take the first step toward earth and hesitate.

For Adam raised his head and called aloud,
"My Father, who has made the garden pall,
Giving me all things and then taking all,
Who with your opposite nature has endowed

Woman, give us your hand for our descent.
Needing us greatly, even in our disgrace,
Guide us, for gladly do we leave this place
For our own land and wished-for banishment."

But woman prayed, "Guide us to Paradise."
Around them slunk the uneasy animals,
Strangely excited, uttering coughs and growls,
And bounded down into the wild abyss.

And overhead the last migrating birds,
Then empty sky. And when the two had gone
A slow half-dozen steps across the stone,
The angel came and stood among the shards

And called them, as though joyously, by name.
They turned in dark amazement and beheld
Eden ablaze with fires of red and gold,
The garden dressed for dying in cold flame,

And it was autumn, and the present world.

And Now, the Weather . . .

The rain that ripens oranges
    Will turn to knifey snow
Up on the sawtooth mountain
    Which we can see below.

The rain that fells the almonds
    Will dust the deserts pale
Have intercourse with Denver
    And then will really sail

To Iowa and Nebraska
    And dump its crystal tons
On all its patriotic
    Motherloving sons

Will cross the Appalachians
    Clasp the industrial murk
And lusting for the Apple
    Layer—at last—New York.

Aubade

What dawn is it?

The morning star stands at the end of your street as you watch
me turn to laugh a kind of goodbye, with love-crazed head
like a white satyr moving through wet bushes.

The morning star bursts in my eye like a hemorrhage as I enter
my car in a dream surrounded by your heavenly-earthly
smell.

The steering wheel is sticky with dew,

The golf course is empty, husbands stir in their sleep desiring,
and though no cocks crow in surburbia, the birds are mak-
ing a hell of a racket.

Into the newspaper dawn as sweet as your arms that hold the old
new world, dawn of green lights that smear the empty
streets with come and go.

It is always dawn when I say goodnight to you,

Dawn of wrecked hair and devastated beds,

Dawn when protective blackness turns to blue and lovers drive
sunward with peripheral vision.

To improvise a little on Villon

Dawn is the end for which we are together.

My house of loaded ashtrays and unwashed glasses, tulip petals
and columbine that spill on the table and splash on the floor,

My house full of your dawns,

My house where your absence is presence,

My slum that loves you, my bedroom of dustmice and cobwebs,
of local paintings and eclectic posters, my bedroom of rust
neckties and divorced mattresses, and of two of your post-
cards, *Pierrot with Flowers* and *Young Girl with Cat,*

My bed where you have thrown your body down like a king's
ransom or a boa constrictor.

But I forgot to say: May passed away last night,

May died in her sleep,

That May that blessed and kept our love in fields and motels.

I erect a priapic statue to that May for lovers to kiss as long as
I'm in print, and polish as smooth as the Pope's toe.

This morning came June of spirea and platitudes,

This morning came June discreetly dressed in gray,
June of terrific promises and lawsuits.

And where are the poems that got lost in the shuffle of spring?
Where is the poem about the eleventh of March, when we raised
    the battleflag of dawn?
Where is the poem about the coral necklace that whipped your
    naked breasts in leaps of love?
The poem concerning the ancient lover we followed through
    your beautiful sleeping head?
The fire-fountain of your earthquake thighs and your electric
    mouth?
Where is the poem about the little one who says my name and
    watches us almost kissing in the sun?
The vellum stretchmarks of your learned belly,
Your rosy-fingered nightgown of nylon and popcorn,
Your razor that caresses your calves like my hands?
Where are the poems that are already obsolete, leaves of last
    month, a very historical month?
Maybe I'll write them, maybe I won't, no matter,
And this is the end for which we are together.
Et c'est la fin pour quoy sommes ensemble.

Bath-Sheba

And I will yet be more vile than thus, and will be base in mine
own sight: and of the maidservants which thou hast spoken of,
of them shall I be had in honor.

I

And it came to pass in the evening
When the heat melts in the sky like lead
And the breeze comes from Baal-Hamon,
King David rose from his purple bed
And walked upon the house-top with a kingly tread.

Into the markets of the town
Into the streets and gateways he looked down
Serene and comely as the evening star,
And there beheld beside a garden path
A woman bending at her bath.

The King gazed, gazed as the sun
On a distant flower, imparting fire.
He touched his messenger and said,
"Bring this woman to my bedstead."
The servant turned and raised his head:
"Lord, shall I to your chamber bring
The wife of the King's man, Uriah,
The wife of a soldier of the King?"

David leaned on the heavy parapet
And spoke not another word.
Ruddy and beautiful is the Lord's man
And a prince's silence can be heard.

2

With wanton eyes Bath-Sheba
That was faithful in her constancy
Lies on the couch of Judah
And luxuriates in adultery.
With nose-rings and silken veils,

Headbands and earrings and tiaras,
With jewelry on her thighs,
Linen and crisping pins,
Tinkle of gold and silver,
Bath-Sheba laughs and sins.
Her girdle too is spicy,
The kiss between her breasts
Henna-flower and hyacinth.
Honey is her nether lip.

He with his cunning harp
And golden hands that slew the bear
Applies his love and beauty,
Binds and unbinds her hair.
The kiss of David savors
Sweetly of myrrh and holiness;
Before their God the lovers
Dress and undress and dress.

The Ark and the Law are embattled
But War and Time are both beguiled;
She sends to say in a letter,
"My Lord, I am with child."

3
At length Uriah by King David brought
To the royal chair, stands and looks pale
And speaks as one from battle, angry, and hot,
Newly released; his thumbs upon his belt
And fingering the proud and studded hilt.
Impatiently he turns and speaks in brief
Of archers fallen, chariots overturned,
Ram-battered towers, and much of running blood,
Friends struck and armor ignominiously
Melted in fire, claimed and fought upon.
To whom the King, quiet and slow of speech,
"Go to thy house and wife; great is your tale,
Great is your journey and your works of blood;
Rest before fighting. Go into thy house."

And now the soldier, white with rage, "O King,
Still in thy tents, the Ark and Israel,
Judah and all abide, and on thy fields
All sway the doubtful outcome of thy God.
For yet the servants of the Almighty stand
Under His captaincy and thine to rule:
Shall I then go into my house and drink,
Lie with my wife and kiss and sleep at noon
But to be taken like a girl alive
Screaming for life and virtue? Now, by my soul
I swear to join my fellows to their last
And fall upon no couches in my death!"

4

King David sealed a letter
And sent it by Uriah's hand
To the chieftain of his armies
That fought to save the Promised Land.

The chieftain read in the letter
That Uriah should wield his sword
In the thick of the hottest battle,
Where he should die for his Lord.

The chieftain wrote to King David
Who lay with Bath-Sheba in a purple bed,
"Abimelech is slain by a woman
And thy servant Uriah also is dead."
King David wrote to his chieftain,
"We fight at the word of Abraham's Lord;
Be courageous and turn the battle
For many and many shall fall by your sword."

But the woman heavily mourned
And wept for Uriah dead.
Not even for the kisses and the words of David
Would she arise and be comforted,
Until King David asked her to wed
And come as a bride to his purple bed,—

And the mourning and the marriage were scarcely done
Before Bath-Sheba bore the King a son.

    5
But Jehovah turned upon his servant David
And struck his child so that it lay
Daily and nightly between life and death,
And David rent his clothes and came to pray.

David lay down on the cold earth.

David ate no food and spoke no word.

David lay for seven days and scarcely stirred.

And on the seventh day the servants came and said,

"Lord David, Lord David, the child is dead."
And they feared his grief.

But the King turned from his tears and rose
And washed and anointed his head
And put on spices and majestic clothes
And worshipped the Lord and ate his bread,
And all the people marveled, but King David said,

"While the child still breathed
I wept and fasted,
For the weight of prayer
Is as gold and fair
In the sight of the Lord;
And my grief has lasted
For seven days
And now the scales are made to yield
And doubt is dead and grief is healed,
I give the Lord praise.
Lay the child upon the sod;
I have felt the hand of God."

And the Lord blessed David with another son,
The greatest of the monarchs, King Solomon.
He wore purple linen; he wore golden shoes;
He was King of the poets, and he ruled the Jews;
He was honored by the nations, the dead and alive;
His songs were a thousand and a thousand and five;
He had a thousand women in a single room;
He built a palace a temple and a golden tomb.
Bath-Sheba was his mother, beautiful to see,
And she lay with King David in adultery.

Buick

As a sloop with a sweep of immaculate wing on her delicate
    spine
And a keel as steel as a root that holds in the sea as she leans,
Leaning and laughing, my warm-hearted beauty, you ride, you
    ride,
You tack on the curves with parabola speed and a kiss of goodbye,
Like a thoroughbred sloop, my new high-spirited spirit, my kiss.

As my foot suggests that you leap in the air with your hips of
    a girl,
My finger that praises your wheel and announces your voices of
    song,
Flouncing your skirts, you blueness of joy, you flirt of politeness,
You leap, you intelligence, essence of wheelness with silvery
    nose,
And your platinum clocks of excitement stir like the hairs of a
    fern.

But how alien you are from the booming belts of your birth
    and the smoke
Where you turned on the stinging lathes of Detroit and Lan-
    sing at night
And shrieked at the torch in your secret parts and the amorous
    tests,
But now with your eyes that enter the future of roads you forget;
You are all instinct with your phosphorous glow and your streak-
    ing hair.

And now when we stop it is not as the bird from the shell that
    I leave
Or the leathery pilot who steps from his bird with a sneer of
    delight,
And not as the ignorant beast do you squat and watch me depart,
But with exquisite breathing you smile, with satisfaction of love,
And I touch you again as you tick in the silence and settle in sleep.

Cadillac

Your luna moths bring poems to my eyes,
Your oriflamme brings banners to my slums;
You are fat and beautiful, rich and ugly,
A boiler with gold leaf floral decorations;
You are a hard plush chair with sloping shoulders
In which Victoria, like a kangaroo,
Raises her blazing arms to a poem by Mr. Tennyson.

In the sewing machine of your mind you mend my flags,
Under your forehead fatted sheep are feeding,
Falcons are climbing at unwritten speeds,
Adding machines are singing your arias,
Your motor playing chess with continents,
With Quincy, Illinois, with Hell, New Jersey,
Halting on Oriental rugs in Fez.
Beautiful are your fine cartouches,
Your organ pipes externalized like tusks.

If only I could put my arm around you,
If only I could look you in the eye,
I would tell you a grave joke about turtles' eggs,
But there are always your ostrich plumes,
The hydrangeas drooping between your breasts.
I am afraid of your prosthetic wrists,
The mason jars of your white corpuscles.

For Christmas I will send you Maeterlinck's *Life of the Bee.*

Priests are praying for your beautiful passengers;
Sacraments are burning in your barley-sugar lighthouses;
You carry wild lawyers over yellow bridges;
Your soul as slow as honey coils in vats.
Voluptuous feather-plated Pegasus,
You carry the horizontal thoughtful dead
To golf greens and to sculpture yards of peace.
On leafy springs, O Love, O Death,
Your footfall is the silence that perfects.

I see you everywhere except in dreams.

Drug Store

I do remember an apothecary,
And hereabouts 'a dwells

It baffles the foreigner like an idiom,
And he is right to adopt it as a form
Less serious than the living-room or bar;
     For it disestablishes the café,
Is a collective, and on basic country.

Not that it praises hygiene and corrupts
The ice-cream parlor and the tobacconist's
Is it a center; but that the attractive symbols
     Watch over puberty and leer
Like rubber bottles waiting for sick-use.

Youth comes to jingle nickels and crack wise;
The baseball scores are his, the magazines
Devoted to lust, the jazz, the Coca-Cola,
     The lending-library of love's latest.
He is the customer; he is heroized.

And every nook and cranny of the flesh
Is spoken to by packages with wiles.
"Buy me, buy me," they whimper and cajole;
     The hectic range of lipstick pouts,
Revealing the wicked and the simple mouth.

With scarcely any evasion in their eye
They smoke, undress their girls, exact a stance;
But only for a moment. The clock goes round;
     Crude fellowships are made and lost;
They slump in booths like rags, not even drunk.

Each in her well-lighted picture window

Each in her well-lighted picture window, reading a book or
   magazine, the Amsterdam whores look quite domestic.
   The canals, as picturesque as expected, add their se-
   renity. The customers stroll from window to window,
   back and forth, comparing merchandise. Where a cur-
   tain is drawn, business is being transacted. These are
   big, fine, strapping whores, heavy in the leg, blonde,
   as is the preference. They don't display their wares, no
   more than crossing a leg. It's like a picture gallery,
   Flemish School, silent through varnish and glaze. What
   detail, what realism of texture, what narrative! And
   look at this masterpiece:

A solid blonde sits in her window at an angle. She appears to
   be looking out, expressionless. Just back of her stands
   an African king in round white hat and lengthy white
   embroidered robe of satin, it may be. Behind him stands
   his servant, very straight. The king's face is a thin and
   noble ebony. And without looking at either African the
   whore holds one hand back of her shoulder, feeling the
   robe of the African king with eloquent fingers, weigh-
   ing the heft of the silk in her thoughtful hand.

Essay on Chess

There are only a few games played by a pair
That are more than games, chess being the most notorious,
Each move signaling an invasion of the other's personality,
    psyche and life-style,
Which is why it is not played by football players, truckdrivers
    or housewives
But by students, physicists, auto-didacts and idiot-savants, as
    many Masters are,
And is raised to Olympic status by cultures that hate one another,
And can never degenerate to the level, say, of "pingpong di-
    plomacy,"
The contest as iffy as the Big Bang or Plato's Cave.

Hours after a game a lover can say to the defeated,
You were only thinking of yourself, that's why you gave up
    your bishop,
And the other may think, if I lose because I love you
It's not intentional. You are better than I am.
But everything said is just another rorschach.
I need a new racquet, the loser jokes, and will buy a new board
Of inlaid wood or cloth-of-silk fit for a rani,
Making it all more formal, like evening dress,
As if it weren't formal enough already.

He muses: I don't want to win from you, I don't want to lose
    to you.
My middle game is strong, almost professional,
But at some point you whistle softly and move right through;
Damn, ineluctable bitch.

Did you know that before the fifteenth century
The queen could only move one square?
Did you know that the king used to jump all over the place
    before he was hobbled?
A hobby horse. All at once the power was hers.
It happened in Europe when they invented love.

The king stands still. Nobody lays a hand on him.
He just stands still in his mutton-chop whiskers, brainless, erect,
Wearing the medals with his own face on them,
His peasants all back in the coffin-box
And a helpless hamstrung horse, ripe for the knackers,
Dying, with crazy beautiful eyes like horse-chestnuts.

He muses: it's only a game invented in Persia
Or some such place that doesn't exist anymore,
And amends this to read—if it were only a game.

The bishops sidle down the avenues, the slippery diplomats with
      their penis-heads.
Those moveable castles like panzers, so modern.
And oh the wild horses leaping over the powers,
You can almost see their delicate legs shrouded in pedestals,
Lifted by fingers of gentle giants.

Kings murdered each other over a chessmatch.
Is says so in the manuals, and all the chess writers call it
A war-game.
              They call it Errors of Appreciation
In the conventicles of war, by actual generals,
With a freudian assumption of an intention to lose.
To Clausewitz the word was Total War,
To Treitschke A Triumph of National Selfhood fit to conquer
      the world,
But all this war talk, Sicilian Defense, the Philador, coign of
      vantage, sphere of action,
The sacrifice, gambit means sacrifice,
All ends in a mate, a word that's not even a pun except in
      English.
Checkmate means *The Shah is dead,*
In chess two queens can never meet,
Two kings can never touch,
And that's the meat of the game, the theory of the play.
The war is only a side-effect of love.

What really matters are the sounds I hear
When you clear the board and put the pieces back in the box,
And the verdict of your eyes when you look up at me.

French Postcard

It is so difficult not to go with it
Once it is seen. It tears the mind agape
With butcher force, with intellectual rape,
And the body hangs by a hair above the pit.

In whose brain, when the order was destroyed,
Did it take form and pose, and when the eye
Clicked, was he guillotined into the void
Where the vile emulsion hangs in strips to dry?

It rose with obvious relish to be viewed,
And lay at a sewer's mouth in the grainy dawn
Where a cop found it. It seemed a platitude
Like a bad postcard of the Parthenon.

I know its family tree, its dossier,
Its memory older than Pompeian walls.
Not that it lives but that it looks at day
Shocks. In the night, wherever it is, it calls,

And never fades, but lies flat and uncurled
Even in the blast furnace at the fire's core,
Feeding fat tallow to our sunken world
Deep in the riches of our father's drawer.

Giantess

When Nature once in lustful hot undress
Conceived gargantuan offspring, then would I
Have loved to live near a young giantess,
Like a voluptuous cat at a queen's feet.

To see her body flower with her desire
And freely spread out in its dreadful play,
Guess if her heart concealed some heavy fire
Whose humid smokes would swim upon her eye;

To feel at leisure her stupendous shapes,
Crawl on the cliffs of her enormous knees,
And, when the unhealthy summer suns fatigued,

Have her stretch out across the plains and so
Sleep in the shadows of her breasts at ease
Like a small hamlet at a mountain's base.

(Baudelaire translation)

Girls Fighting, Broadway

How beautiful it is,
that eye-on-the-object look.

two girls one blond one latin with fixed hair
in summer dresses hug each other
in a shallow doorway shove each other

as if playfully on streaming Broadway
in heavy August it looks like kissing
to a passerby or some kind of come-on

till a scream retches into the traffic
and heads turn and they are down
on the polluted sidewalk clawing and ripping

and hurling fuck heads striking concrete
thighs open to faces a handsome man
in striped underwear pulls them apart

and is struck backwards a crowd collects
clerks lean out of shops a circle forms
as at a cockfight where feathers fly

and flecks of blood spit through space
they are using teeth and nails and fists
the latin screaming and the blond showing

gold teeth in her open mouth and grabbing
a fallen shoe and swinging hard at
the latin's face they stand they sway they fall

again on the dog-smear and mash of the sidewalk
roiling like lovers spilling over with lust
strong men stand by with burning studious faces

mature women bump their hips to the front
as at a roller-derby while the girls
lurch to their feet between rounds

hissing and panting and heaving in their wet
their passionate pure oblivion

Glass Poem

The afternoon lies glazed upon the wall
And on the window shines the scene-like bay,
And on the dark reflective floor a ray
Falls, and my thoughts like ashes softly fall.

And I look up as one who looks through glass
And sees the thing his soul clearly desires,
Who stares until his vision flags and tires,
But from whose eye the image fails to pass;

Until a wish crashes the vitreous air
And comes to your real hands across this space,
Thief-like and deeply cut to touch your face,
Dearly, most bitterly to touch your hair.

And I could shatter these transparent lights,
Could thrust my arms and bring your body through,
Break from the subtle spectrum the last hue
And change my eyes to dark soft-seeing nights.

But the sun stands and the hours stare like brass
And day flows thickly into permanent time,
And toward your eyes my threatening wishes climb
Where you move through a sea of solid glass.

Homewreck

By and large there is no blood,
Police reports to the contrary notwithstanding,
But lots of ichor, a few missing books,
A hasty and disproportionate money transaction
And a sudden enlargement of space.

Three parties form the usual cast,
One happy, one in a rage, and one in the wings,
A telephone rings and rings and rings,
Incinerators open and close and open
And the dramatis personae have all lost face

Though they themselves don't think so
Or try not to think so because the immediate public
Is immediately involved,
Greedy to know what kind of problem is solved
By a seriously departing suitcase.

The public waits for the party in the wings
Who is no longer incognito, who
Has achieved stardom in a matinee
And appears shyly to complete the play
And just as shyly is proferred—an ashtray.

Love for a Hand

Two hands lie still, the hairy and the white,
And soon down ladders of reflected light
The sleepers climb in silence. Gradually
They separate on paths of long ago,
Each winding on his arm the unpleasant clew
That leads, live as a nerve, to memory.

But often when too steep her dream descends,
Perhaps to the grotto where her father bends
To pick her up, the husband wakes as though
He had forgotten something in the house.
Motionless he eyes the room that glows
With the little animals of light that prowl

This way and that. Soft are the beasts of light
But softer still her hand that drifts so white
Upon the whiteness. How like a water-plant
It floats upon the black canal of sleep,
Suspended upward from the distant deep
In pure achievement of its lovely want!

Quietly then he plucks it and it folds
And is again a hand, small as a child's.
He would revive it but it barely stirs
And so he carries it off a little way
And breaks it open gently. Now he can see
The sweetness of the fruit, his hand eats hers.

Mongolian Idiot

A dog that spoke, a monster born of sheep
We mercilessly kill, and kill the thought,
Yet house the parrot and let the centaur go,
These being to their nature and those not.
We laugh at apes, that never quite succeed
   At eating soup or wearing hats.

Adam had named so many but not this,
This that would name a curse when it had come,
Unfinished man, or witch, or myth, or sin,
Not ever father and never quite a son.
Ape had outstripped him, dog and darling lamb
   And all the kindergarten beasts.

Enter the bare room of his mind and count
His store of words with letters large and black;
See how he handles clumsily those blocks
With swans and sums; his colored picture books.
At thirty-five he squeals to see the ball
   Bounce in the air and roll away.

Pity and fear we give this innocent
Who maimed his mother's beautiful instinct;
But she would say, "My body had a dog;
I bore the ape and nursed the crying sheep.
He is my kindness and my splendid gift
   Come from all life and for all life."

Morning

I'm awake before you. I wait for you to appear.
You appear like a sunburst. My heart flies open
I burgeon all over like the Garden of Eden.

You are in the garden looking for roses
You are in the kitchen dripping your coffee
    munching bread and cheese.
You are reading *The Times*.
You are giving me a lecture on Reagan.

My eyes follow you like a cop-car.
No wonder you close your door.
Last night I came to talk about Auden,
    the fascinating textual problems.
Your light was out.
Only the *yahrzeit* candle for your mother flickered.

I wait for you in the morning.
When the day of my life begins.

My Grandmother

My grandmother moves to my mind in context of sorrow
And, as if apprehensive of near death, in black;
Whether erect in chair, her dry and corded throat harangued
    by grief,
Or at ragged book bent in Hebrew prayer,
Or gentle, submissive, and in tears to strangers;
Whether in sunny parlor or back of drawn blinds.

Though time and tongue made any love disparate,
On daguerreotype with classic perspective
Beauty I sigh and soften at is hers.
I pity her life of deaths, the agony of her own,
But most that history moved her through
Stranger lands and many houses,
Taking her exile for granted, confusing
The tongues and tasks of her children's children.

Office Love

Office love, love of money and fight, love of calculated sex.
The offices reek with thin volcanic metal. Tears fall in
typewriters like drops of solder. Brimstone of bras-
siers, low voices, the whirr of dead-serious play. From
the tropical tree and the Rothko in the Board Room to
the ungrammatical broom closet fragrant with waxes,
to the vast typing pool where coffee is being served by
dainty waitresses maneuvering their hand trucks, music
almost unnoticeable falls. The very telephones are hard
and kissable, the electric water cooler sweetly sweats.
Gold simmers to a boil in braceleted and sunburned
cheeks. What ritual politeness nevertheless, what sub-
tlety of clothing. And if glances meet, if shoulders graze,
there's no harm done. Flowers, celebrations, pregnancy
leave, how the little diamonds sparkle under the psycho-
logically soft-colored ceilings. It's an elegant windowless
world of soft pressures and efficiency joys, of civilized
mishaps—mere runs in the stocking, papercuts.

Where the big boys sit the language is rougher. Phone calls to
China and a private shower. No paper visible anywhere.
Policy is decided by word of mouth like gangsters. There
the power lies and is sexless.

Premises

Moving must be in our nature
    As Heraclitus wrote;
We clamber around the landscape
    Lightfooted as the goat

Taking our premises lightly
    But not our creative acts
Our lares two old typewriters
    But never the artifacts

Which you place around to perfection
    Ensconce them I don't know how
Ceramics and plants and baskets.
    Is the Rothko poster—Horchow?

Aware of the dangers of homing
    Of loading the chambers with crap
We avoid acquisitions like poison
    "Decorating the trap."

May our walls be nunnish, monastic,
    Our only ikon the sky
Except for books by the thousands
    And no *horror vacui.*

The Back

One of the foremost organs of beauty
Especially in women, spaceful and pure
A sky of skin uninterrupted
By mountain-tops and grots
Swamps, fens, rocks, trees
And serpents in gardens: the back.

A roseate fragrance endews it
It gleams like an Australian moon
And is no moor of thatch and thorn
But a mile-wide river of veldt
Mile-wide and fraction-deep like the Platte
Where no man lives, a lone terrain,
And luxuriates in itself
And is the very mirage of beauty
To which even whispering is audibly loud
And there are no antries.

On this small platonic continent
Let love graze.

The Bathers

Man and woman, they enter the sea,
The animal-blue, the bovine slippery wave
That, rising, bares its corrugations
And, falling, takes them in its silky teeth
Tightly, while the vast body mills around
Their already watery bodies, till, half blind,
They pass invisibly through its bony sheath,
Swallowed alive and gasping and let go.

They do not even hear the crash of it
Behind them, where it wrecks itself on land,
But are already willed by water,
Weightless and far gone in forgetfulness.

And they are born in that unrisen sky
Out there where all is bright and water-galled
And the loose guts of water tangle them
And then dissolve; where only the dead wave
Comes back awhile, dissipated
And scattered on the wide wash of the sea.

The bathers, blissful in primeval tears,
Forgotten even by the sea itself
That rocks them absently, two bobbing heads,
Onions or oranges
Dumped by the freight of summer on the sea.

They lose even the power of speech;
They must go back to learn;
They make the difficult return
Where nets of water hold them, feel their legs,
Cast ropes of coldness round their bellies,
Trip them, throw gravel at their ankles,
Until, unpredictably, the entire sea
Makes them a path and gives them a push to the beach.

And they lie down between the yellow boats
Where the sun comes and picks them out
And rubs its fire into their sea-pale flesh,
Rubbing their blood, licking their heavy hair,
Breathing upon their words with drying fire.

The First Time

Behind shut doors, in shadowy quarantine,
There shines the lamp of iodine and rose
That stains all love with its medicinal bloom.
This boy, who is no more than seventeen,
Not knowing what to do, takes off his clothes
As one might in a doctor's anteroom.

Then in a cross-draft of fear and shame
Feels love hysterically burn away,
A candle swimming down to nothingness
Put out by its own wetted gusts of flame,
And he stands smooth as uncarved ivory
Heavily curved for some expert caress.

And finally sees the always open door
That is invisible till the time has come,
And half falls through as through a rotten wall
To where chairs twist with dragons from the floor
And the great bed drugged with its own perfume
Spreads its carnivorous flower-mouth for all.

The girl is sitting with her back to him;
She wears a black thing and she rakes her hair,
Hauling her round face upward like moonrise;
She is younger than he, her angled arms are slim
And like a country girl her feet are bare.
She watches him behind her with old eyes,

Transfixing him in space like some grotesque,
Far, far from her where he is still alone
And being here is more and more untrue.
Then she turns round, as one turns at a desk,
And looks at him, too naked and too soon,
And almost gently asks: *Are you a Jew?*

The Figurehead

Watching my paralytic friend
Caught in the giant clam of himself
Fast on the treacherous shoals of his bed,
I look away to the place he had left
Where at a decade's distance he appeared
To pause in his walk and think of a limp.
One day he arrived at the street bearing
The news that he dragged an ancient foot:
The people on their porches seemed to sway.

Though there are many wired together
In this world and the next, my friend
Strains in his clamps. He is all sprung
And locked in the rust of inner change.
The therapist who plucks him like a harp
Is a cold torture: the animal bleats
And whimpers on its far seashore
As she leans to her find with a smooth hunger.

Somewhere in a storm my pity went down:
It was a wooden figurehead
With sea-hard breasts and polished mouth.
But women wash my friend with brine
From shallow inlets of their eyes,
And women rock my friend with waves
That pulsate from the female moon.
They gather at his very edge and haul
My driftwood friend toward their fires.

Speaking of dancing, joking of sex,
I watch my paralytic friend
And seek my pity in those wastes where he
Becomes my bobbing figurehead.
Then as I take my leave I wade
Loudly into the shallows of his pain,
I splash like a vacationer,
I scare his legs and stir the time of day
With rosy clouds of sediment.

The House

We walked over here when it was summer field
And every tree for acres had been felled.
A tumbleweed, the roundness of the world
Steered close to us and ferried up the hill.
We walked to the dark sill of the excavation
And crossed elastic planks above the pit;
There was impressionable paving, open pipe.
We passed within the cage of wooden ribs,
Gleaming with nails all pointing straight at us.
We ducked through vines of poison-colored wires,
Past the bathtub like a sarcophagus
Crated. Masons were clinking spotless bricks
Pragmatically. We opened the first door,
As a man opens a safe deposit box.
We walked on sod covering the earthen wound;
Squares of live rug gave underfoot like flesh.
Keys were mated with reluctant locks.
Current set up its brilliant nervous system.
We walked on wisps of blond excelsior
And read crimped headlines out of packing cases.
We caught three mice in the acoustical tile;
Three little backs were broken on quick springs.
We sawed and tacked and swept and kissed and cursed
And laid in books and wood and bought a set
Of aluminum numbers and shaved the gray new glass
With razor blades. We slept in whited smells,
Undressed uncurtained in a treeless world.

The Second-Best Bed

In the name of the almighty God, amen,
   I, William Shakespeare, take my pen
   And do bequeath in perfect health
To Christ my soul and to my kin my wealth
      When I am dead.
      And to Anne, good dame,
      I bequeath my name,
A table, a chair, and the second-best bed.

To Judith a hundred fifty pounds I give,
   The same if three more years she live,
   And the broad-edge silver bowl. To Joan
My hose and clothes and all the suits I own
      Both blue and red.
      And to Anne, good dame,
      I bequeath my name,
A table, a chair, and the second-best bed.

Ten pounds to beggars for their drink and board,
   To Mr. Thomas Cole my sword,
   To Richard Burbage, Cundell, Nash,
Heminge and Hamlet one pound six in cash,
      And to her I wed
      Who is Anne, good dame,
      I bequeath my name,
A table, a chair, and the second-best bed.

To Joan also my Stratford house I will,
   For sisters shall not go with nil,
   And to her sons five pounds apiece
To be paid within a year of my decease.
      And as I have said
      To Anne, good dame,
      I bequeath my name,
A table, a chair, and the second-best bed.

Last, to my daughter, born Susanna Hall,
 My barns and stables, lands and all,
 Tenements, orchards, jewels, and wares,
All these forever for herself and heirs,
 Till all are dead;
 But to Anne, good dame,
A table, a chair, and the second-best bed.

Good wife, bad fortune is to blame
That I bequeath, when I am dead,
To you my honor and my name,
A table, a chair, and the second-best bed.

The Spider Mums

The spider mums are yellow
In the chill green room.
Six days from the florist
And standing center stage—
How well they hold their age!

Crystals dropped in water
Perpetuate the bloom
Like Stendhal's twigs of diamonds
Created overnight
Of ancient salt and light.

Essays on time get nowhere
But back where they began.
Still, crystalization
Can be the first in art
Though permanent flowers aren't.

V-Letter

I love you first because your face is fair,
      Because your eyes Jewish and blue,
Set sweetly with the touch of foreignness
Above the cheekbones, stare rather than dream.
Often your countenance recalls a boy
      Blue-eyed and small, whose silent mischief
Tortured his parents and compelled my hate
      To wish his ugly death.
Because of this reminder, my soul's trouble,
And for your face, so often beautiful,
      I love you, wish you life.

I love you first because you wait, because
      For your own sake, I cannot write
Beyond these words. I love you for these words
That sting and creep like insects and leave filth.
I love you for the poverty you cry
      And I bend down with tears of steel
That melt your hand like wax, not for this war
      The droplets shattering
Those candle-glowing fingers of my joy,
But for your name of agony, my love,
      That cakes my mouth with salt.

And all your imperfections and perfections
      And all your magnitude of grace
And all this love explained and unexplained
Is just a breath. I see you woman-size
And this looms larger and more goddess-like
      Than silver goddesses on screens.
I see you in the ugliness of light,
      Yet you are beautiful,
And in the dark of absence your full length
Is such as meets my body to the full
      Though I am starved and huge.

You turn me from these days as from a scene
      Out of an open window far
Where lies the foreign city and the war.
You are my home and in your spacious love
I dream to march as under flaring flags
      Until the door is gently shut.
Give me the tearless lesson of your pride,
      Teach me to live and die
As one deserving anonymity,
The mere devotion of a house to keep
      A woman and a man.

Give me the free and poor inheritance
      Of our own kind, not furniture
Of education, nor the prophet's pose,
The general cause of words, the hero's stance,
The ambitions incommensurable with flesh,
      But the drab makings of a room
Where sometimes in the afternoon of thought
      The brief and blinding flash
May light the enormous chambers of your will
And show the gracious Parthenon that time
      Is ever measured by.

As groceries in a pantry gleam and smile
      Because they are important weights
Bought with the metal minutes of your pay,
So do these hours stand in solid rows,
The dowry for a use in common life.
      I love you first because your years
Lead to my matter-of-fact and simple death
      Or to our open marriage,
And I pray nothing for my safety back,
Not even luck, because our love is whole
      Whether I live or fail.

Waitress

Whoever with the compasses of his eyes
Is plotting the voyage of your steady shape
As you come laden through the room and back
And rounding your even bottom like a Cape
Crooks his first finger, whistles through his lip
Till you arrive, all motion, like a ship,

He is my friend—consider his dark pangs
And love of Niger, naked indigence,
Dance him the menu of a poem and squirm
Deep in the juke-box jungle, green and dense.
Surely he files his teeth, punctures his nose,
Carves out the god and takes off all his clothes.

For once, the token on the table's edge
Sufficing, proudly and with hair unpinned
You mounted the blueplate, stretched out and grinned
Like Christmas fish and turkey pink and skinned,
Eyes on the half-shell, loin with parsley stuck,
Thigh-bones and ribs and little toes to suck.

I speak to you, ports of the northern myth,
This dame is carved and eaten. One by one,
God knows what hour, her different parts go home,
Lastly her pants, and day or night is done;
But on the restaurant the sign of fear
Reddens and blazes—"English spoken here."

WAR

Auto Wreck

Its quick soft silver bell beating, beating,
And down the dark one ruby flare
Pulsing out red light like an artery,
The ambulance at top speed floating down
Past beacons and illuminated clocks
Wings in a heavy curve, dips down,
And brakes speed, entering the crowd.
The doors leap open, emptying light;
Stretchers are laid out, the mangled lifted
And stowed into the little hospital.
Then the bell, breaking the hush, tolls once,
And the ambulance with its terrible cargo
Rocking, slightly rocking, moves away,
As the door, an afterthought, are closed.

We are deranged, walking among the cops
Who sweep glass and are large and composed.
One is still making notes under the light.
One with a bucket douches ponds of blood
Into the street and gutter.
One hangs lanterns on the wrecks that cling,
Empty husks of locusts, to iron poles.

Our throats were tight as tourniquets,
Our feet were bound with splints, but now,
Like convalescents intimate and gauche,
We speak through sickly smiles and warn
With the stubborn saw of common sense,
The grim joke and the banal resolution.
The traffic moves around with care,
But we remain, touching a wound
That opens to our richest horror.
Already old, the question Who shall die?
Becomes unspoken Who is innocent?
For death in war is done by hands;
Suicide has cause and stillbirth, logic;
And cancer, simple as a flower, blooms.

But this invites the occult mind,
Cancels our physics with a sneer,
And spatters all we knew of denouement
Across the expedient and wicked stones.

California Petrarchan

I hear the sunset ambulances surround
Suburbia at the turquoise edge of day,
Loping along the not-too-far freeway
Where olive trees and red bloodshed abound.
The oleanders with a shore-like sound
Perform their dance beside my own driveway
As if they also had a word to say
In all their whiteness beautifully gowned.

This Italy with insanity all its own
Lacks only history to make it true
And bitterness that ripens hour by hour.
This baby Italy, more straw than stone,
Stumbling, choking, fighting toward the New,
Bursts into flame with its own fire power.

Elegy for a Dead Soldier

I

A white sheet on the tail-gate of a truck
Becomes an altar; two small candlesticks
Sputter at each side of the crucifix
Laid round with flowers brighter than the blood,
Red as the red of our apocalypse,
Hibiscus that a marching man will pluck
To stick into his rifle or his hat,
And great blue morning-glories pale as lips
That shall no longer taste or kiss or swear.
The wind begins a low magnificat,
The chaplain chats, the palmtrees swirl their hair,
The columns come together through the mud.

II

We too are ashes as we watch and hear
The psalm, the sorrow, and the simple praise
Of one whose promised thoughts of other days
Were such as ours, but now wholly destroyed,
The service record of his youth wiped out,
His dream dispersed by shot, must disappear.
What can we feel but wonder at a loss
That seems to point at nothing but the doubt
Which flirts our sense of luck into the ditch?
Reader of Paul who prays beside this fosse,
Shall we believe our eyes or legends rich
With glory and rebirth beyond the void?

III

For this comrade is dead, dead in the war,
A young man out of millions yet to live,
One cut away from all that war can give,
Freedom of self and peace to wander free.
Who mourns in all this sober multiude
Who did not feel the bite of it before
The bullet found its aim? This worthy flesh,
This boy laid in a coffin and reviewed—

Who has not wrapped himself in the same flag,
Heard the light fall of dirt, his wound still fresh,
Felt his eyes closed, and heard the distant brag
Of the last volley of humanity?

IV

By chance I saw him die, stretched on the ground,
A tattooed arm lifted to take the blood
Of someone else sealed in a tin. I stood
During the last delirium that stays
The intelligence a tiny moment more,
And then the strangulation, the last sound.
The end was sudden, like a foolish play,
A stupid fool slamming a foolish door,
The absurd catastrophe, half-prearranged,
And all the decisive things still left to say.
So we disbanded, angrier and unchanged,
Sick with the utter silence of dispraise.

V

We ask for no statistics of the killed,
For nothing political impinges on
This single casualty, or all those gone,
Missing or healing, sinking or dispersed,
Hundreds of thousands counted, millions lost.
More than an accident and less than willed
Is every fall, and this one like the rest.
However others calculate the cost,
To us the final aggregate is *one*,
One with a name, one transferred to the blest;
And though another stoops and takes the gun,
We cannot add the second to the first.

VI

I would not speak for him who could not speak
Unless my fear were true: he was not wronged,
He knew to which decision he belonged
But let it choose itself. Ripe in instinct,
Neither the victim nor the volunteer,

55

He followed, and the leaders could not seek
Beyond the followers. Much of this he knew;
The journey was a detour that would steer
Into the Lincoln Highway of a land
Remorselessly improved, excited, new,
And that was what he wanted. He had planned
To earn and drive. He and the world had winked.

VII

No history deceived him, for he knew
Little of times and armies not his own;
He never felt that peace was but a loan,
Had never questioned the idea of gain.
Beyond the headlines once or twice he saw
The gathering of a power by the few
But could not tell their names; he cast his vote,
Distrusting all the elected but not law.
He laughed at socialism; *on mourrait*
Pour les industriels? He shed his coat
And not for brotherhood, but for his pay.
To him the red flag marked the sewer main.

VIII

Above all else he loathed the homily,
The slogan and the ad. He paid his bill,
But not for Congressmen at Bunker Hill.
Ideals were few and those there were not made
For conversation. He belonged to church
But never spoke of God. The Christmas tree,
The Easter egg, baptism, he observed,
Never denied the preacher on his perch,
And would not sign Resolved That or Whereas.
Softness he had and hours and nights reserved
For thinking, dressing, dancing to the jazz.
His laugh was real, his manners were homemade.

IX

Of all men poverty pursued him least;
He was ashamed of all the down and out,

Spurned the panhandler like an uneasy doubt,
And saw the unemployed as a vague mass
Incapable of hunger or revolt.
He hated other races, south or east,
And shoved them to the margin of his mind.
He could recall the justice of the Colt,
Take interest in a gang-war like a game.
His ancestry was somewhere far behind
And left him only his peculiar name.
Doors opened, and he recognized no class.

x

His children would have known a heritage,
Just or unjust, the richest in the world,
The quantum of all art and science curled
In the horn of plenty, bursting from the horn,
A people bathed in honey, Paris come,
Vienna transferred with the highest wage,
A World's Fair spread to Phoenix, Jacksonville,
Earth's capital, the new Byzantium,
Kingdom of man—who knows? Hollow or firm,
No man can ever prophesy until
Out of our death some undiscovered germ,
Whole toleration or pure peace is born.

XI

The time to mourn is short that best becomes
The military dead. We lift and fold the flag,
Lay bare the coffin with its written tag,
And march away. Behind, four others wait
To lift the box the heaviest of loads.
The anesthetic afternoon benumbs,
Sickens our senses, forces back our talk.
We know that others on tomorrow's roads
Will fall, ourselves perhaps, the man beside,
Over the world the threatened, all who walk:
And could we mark the grave of him who died
We would write this beneath his name and date:

EPITAPH

Underneath this wooden cross there lies
A Christian killed in battle. You who read,
Remember that this stranger died in pain;
And passing here, if you can lift your eyes
Upon a peace kept by a human creed,
Know that one soldier has not died in vain.

Full Moon: New Guinea

These nights we fear the aspects of the moon,
Sleep lightly in the radiance falling clear
On palms and ferns and hills and us; for soon
The small burr of the bombers in our ear
Tickles our rest; we rise as from a nap
And take our helmets absently and meet,
Prepared for any spectacle or mishap,
At trenches fresh and narrow at our feet.

Look up, look up, and wait and breathe. These nights
We fear Orion and the Cross. The crowd
Of deadly insects caught in our long lights
Glitter and seek to burrow in a cloud
Soft-minded with high explosive. Breathe and wait,
The bombs are falling darkly for our fate.

Grant's Tomb Revisited

Something unkempt about it
As if the tomb itself were moribund,
Sepulchre of our own Napoleon,
Litter fluttering under the battleflags
And few white faces.
We've all seen better days,
Hiram Ulysses.
They say the neighborhood is in transition
And only the Hudson keeps an even keel.

The stocky tower rises dirtily,
Imperial, republican,
With sculptures all wrong for today.
I'm puzzled why you like this place.
Pose me under the big stone eagle
Amidst the sociological decay.

Who collared this mausoleum with bright tiles,
Flashing, swooping childwork of the age,
Leaping around like a Luna Park?
Take my picture under the Mirò arch,
A neighborhood Mirò, not so bad at that.

Let's go upstairs, that's what it's all about
Where only a single guard remains inside
And seems almost surprised to see
Only two visitors, not in a group.

"One million people turned out for the event
"Buildings all over the city draped in black
"Sixty thousand marchers up Broadway
"Stretched seven miles, the President
"Cabinet, Supreme Court, almost the entire Congress
"Ships on the Hudson fired a salute

And there below
The two monogamous crypts

Eight and a half tons each
From the days when there was no doubt
About the reciprocity of might,
The General on the left and Julia on the right.

Homecoming

Lost in the vastness of the void Pacific
My thousand days of exile, pain,
Bid me farewell. Gone is the Southern Cross
To her own sky, fallen a continent
Under the wave, dissolved the bitterest isles
In their salt element,
And here upon the deck the mist encloses
My smile that would light up all darkness
And ask forgiveness of the things that thrust
Shame and all death on millions and on me.

We bring no raw materials from the East
But green-skinned men in blue-lit holds
And lunatics impounded between-decks;
The mighty ghoul-ship that we ride exhales
The sickly-sweet stench of humiliation,
And even the majority, untouched by steel
Or psychoneurosis, stare with eyes in rut,
Their hands a rabble to snatch the riches
Of glittering shops and girls.

Because I am angry at this kindness which
It both habitual and contradictory
To the life of armies, now I stand alone
And hate the swarms of khaki men that crawl
Like lice upon the wrinkled hide of earth,
Infesting ships as well. Not otherwise
Could I lean outward piercing fog to find
Our sacred bridge of exile and return.
My tears are psychological, not poems
To the United States; my smile is prayer.

Gnawing the thin slops of anxiety,
Escorted by the ground swell and by gulls,
In silence and with mystery we enter
The territorial waters. Not till then
Does that convulsive terrible joy, more sudden

And brilliant than the explosion of a ship,
Shatter the tensions of the heaven and sea
To crush a hundred thousand skulls
And liberate in that high burst of love
The imprisoned souls of soldiers and of me.

Hospital

Inside or out, the key is pain. It holds
The florist to your pink medicinal rose,
The nickname to the corpse. One wipes it from
Blue German blades or drops it down the drain;
The novelist with a red tube up his nose
Gingerly pets it. Nurse can turn it off.

This is the Oxford of all sicknesses.
Kings have lain here and fabulous small Jews
And actresses whose legs were always news.
In this black room the painter lost his sight,
The crippled dancer here put down her shoes,
And the scholar's memory broke, like an old clock.

These reached to heaven and inclined their heads
While starchy angels reached them into beds:
These stooped to hell to labor out their time,
Or choked to death in seas of glaucous slime:
All tasted fire, and then, their hate annealed,
Ate sad ice-cream and wept upon a child.

What church is this, what factory of souls
Makes the bad good and fashions a new nose,
And the doctors reel with Latin and even the dead
Expect the unexpected? For O the souls
Fly back like heavy homing-birds to roost
In long-racked limbs, filling the lonely boughs.

The dead cry *life* and stagger up the hill;
But is there still the incorrigible city where
The well enjoy their poverty and the young
Worship the gutter? Is Wednesday still alive
And Tuesday wanting terribly to sin?
Hush, there are many pressing the oak doors,

Saying, "Are boys and girls important fears?
Can you predict the elections by my guts?"

But the rubber gloves are deep in a deep wound,
Stitching a single heart. These far surpass
Themselves, their wives, and the removed goitre;
Are, for the most part, human but unbandaged.

Midnight Show

The year is done, the last act of the vaudeville,
The last top hat and patent leather tappity-tap
Enclosed in darkness. Pat. Blackout. Only the organ
Groans, groans, its thousand golden throats in love;
While blue lowlight suffuses mysteries of sleep
Through racks of heads, and smoothly parts the gauzy veil
That slips, the last pretense of peace, into the wings.

With a raucous crash the music rises to its feet,
And pouring from the hidden eye like God the Light
The light white-molten cold fills out the vacant field
With shattered cities, striped ships, and maps with lines
That crawl—symbols of horror, symbols of obscenity;
A girl astride a giant cannon, holding a flag;
Removal of stone and stained-glass saints from a known
        cathedral;

And the Voice, the loving and faithful pointer, trots beside
Reel after reel, taking death in its well-trained stride.
The Voice, the polite, the auctioneer, places his hints
Like easy bids. The lab assistant, the Voice, dips
Their pity like litmus papers into His rancid heart.—
Dream to be surfeited, nerves clogged up with messages,
And, backed up at the ganglion, the news refused.

Dream to be out in snow where every corner Santa,
Heart of one generation's dreams, tinkles a bell.
We know him too. He is the Unemployed, but clowns
As the Giver, receiving pennies in a cast-iron pot.
Dream to be cold with Byrd at the world's bottom. Dream
To be warm in the Vatican, photographing a manuscript.
Dream to be there, a cell in Europe's poisoned blood.

Revulsion cannot rouse our heads for pride or protest.
The eye sees as the camera, a clean moronic gaze,
And to go is not impossible but merely careless.

O wife, what shall we tell the children that we saw?
O son, what shall we tell our father? And O my friend,
What shall we tell our senses when the lights go up
And noiselessly the golden curtains crash together!

Nostalgia

My soul stands at the window of my room,
    And I ten thousand miles away;
My days are filled with Ocean's sound of doom,
    Salt and cloud and the bitter spray.
Let the wind blow, for many a man shall die.

My selfish youth, my books with gilded edge,
    Knowledge and all gaze down the street;
The potted plants upon the window ledge
    Gaze down with selfish lives and sweet.
Let the wind blow, for many a man shall die.

My night is now her day, my day her night,
    So I lie down, and so I rise;
The sun burns close, the star is losing height,
    The clock is hunted down the skies.
Let the wind blow, for many a man shall die.

Truly a pin can make the memory bleed,
    A word explode the inward mind
And turn the skulls and flowers never freed
    Into the air, no longer blind.
Let the wind blow, for many a man shall die.

Laughter and grief join hands. Always the heart
    Clumps in the breast with heavy stride;
The face grows lined and wrinkled like a chart,
    The eyes bloodshot with tears and tide.
Let the wind blow, for many a man shall die.

Of love and death in the Garrison State I sing

Of love and death in the Garrison State I sing. From uni-
formed populations rises the High Art, *Oedipus King*,
the Nō, the ballerina bleeding in her slippers. At the
Officer's Club adultery is rationed (their children are
not allowed to play with guns; this helps whet their
appetite). The ladies are discussing the chemical con-
trol of behavior by radio waves: that will solve the
problem of neighbors. Symposia on causes of desertion
draw record-breaking crowds. The handsomer pacifists
are invited to the most sought-after cocktail parties. The
women try their hand at them in the rumpus room;
some progress reported. Waves of asceticism sweep the
automobile industry. The mere sight of a Sam Browne
belt, which used to inspire contempt, brings tears to the
eyes of high-school boys. All flabby citizens are auto-
matically put under surveillance. Chess problems super-
sede crap in the noncoms' barracks. The sacred number
is Two: two parties, two powers sworn to mutual death,
two poles of everything from ethics to magnetics. It's
a balanced society.

Today the order goes out: all distant places are to be abolished:
beachcombers are shot like looters. Established poets are
forced to wear beards and bluejeans; they are treated
kindly in bohemian zoos; mysterious stipends drift their
way. They can trade soap for peyote at specified libraries.
Children's prizes are given for essays on the pleasures of
crisis. Historians are awarded all the key posts in the
foreign office. Sculptors who use old shrapnel are made
the heads of schools of design. Highways move under-
ground like veins of ore. The Anti-Sky Association (vol-
unteer contributions only) meets naked at high noon
and prays for color blindness.

"Color is a biological luxury."

Quintana lay in the shallow grave of coral

Quintana lay in the shallow grave of coral. The guns boomed stupidly fifty yards away. The plasma trickled into his arm. Naked and filthy, covered with mosquitoes, he looked at me as I read his white cloth tag. How do you feel, Quintana? He looks away from my gaze. I lie: we'll get you out of here sometime today.

I never saw him again, dead or alive. Skin and bones, with eyes as soft as soot, neck long as a thigh, a cross on his breast-bone not far from the dog tags. El Greco was all I could think of. Quintana lying in his shallow foxhole wait-ing to be evacuated. A dying man with a Spanish name equals El Greco. A truck driver from Dallas probably.

When the Japs were making the banzai charge, to add insult to death, they came at us screaming the supreme insult: *Babe Ruth, go to hell!* The Americans, on the other hand, when the Japs flew over dropping sticks of ex-plosives, shouted into the air, as if they could hear: *Tojo, eat shit!*

Soldiers fall in love with the enemy all too easily. It's the allies they hate. Every war is its own excuse. That's why they're all surrounded with ideals. That's why they're all crusades.

Scyros

snuffle and sniff and handkerchief

The doctor punched my vein
The captain called me Cain
Upon my belly sat the sow of fear
  With coins on either eye
  The President came by
And whispered to the braid what none could hear

High over where the storm
Stood steadfast cruciform
The golden eagle sank in wounded wheels
  White Negroes laughing still
  Crept fiercely on Brazil
Turning the navies upward on their keels

Now one by one the trees
Stripped to their naked knees
To dance upon the heaps of shrunken dead
  The roof of England fell
  Great Paris tolled her bell
And China staunched her milk and wept for bread

No island singly lay
But lost its name that day
The Ainu dived across the plunging sands
  From dawn to dawn to dawn
  King George's birds came on
Strafing the tulips from his children's hands

Thus in the classic sea
Southeast from Thessaly
The dynamited mermen washed ashore
  And tritons dressed in steel
  Trolled heads with rod and reel
And dredged potatoes from the Aegean floor

Hot is the sky and green
Where Germans have been seen
The moon leaks metal on the Atlantic fields
Pink boys in birthday shrouds
Loop lightly through the clouds
Or coast the peaks of Finland on their shields

That prophet year by year
Lay still but could not hear
Where scholars tapped to find his new remains
Gog and Magog ate pork
In vertical New York
And war began next Wednesday on the Danes

The Dome of Sunday

With focus sharp as Flemish-painted face
In film of varnish brightly fixed
And through a polished hand-lens deeply seen,
Sunday at noon through hyaline thin air
Sees down the street,
And in the camera of my eye depicts
Row-houses and row-lives:
Glass after glass, door after door the same,
Face after face the same, the same,
The brutal visibility the same;

As if one life emerging from one house
Would pause, a single image caught between
Two facing mirrors where vision multiplies
Beyond perspective,
A silent clatter in the high-speed eye
Spinning out photo-circulars of sight.

I see slip to the curb the long machines
Out of whose warm and windowed rooms pirouette
Shellacked with silk and light
The hard legs of our women.
Our women are one woman, dressed in black.
The carmine printed mouth
And cheeks as soft as muslin-glass belong
Outright to one dark dressy man,
Merely a swagger at her curvy side.
This is their visit to themselves:
All day from porch to porch they weave
A nonsense pattern through the even glare,
Stealing in surfaces
Cold vulgar glances at themselves.

And high up in the heated room all day
I wait behind the plate glass pane for one,
Hot as a voyeur for a glimpse of one,
The vision to blot out this woman's sheen;

All day my sight records expensively
Row-houses and row-lives.

But nothing happens; no diagonal
With melting shadow falls across the curb:
Neither the blinded negress lurching through fatigue,
Nor exiles bleeding from their pores,
Nor that bright bomb slipped lightly from its rack
To splinter every silvered glass and crystal prism,
Witch-bowl and perfume bottle
And billion candle-power dressing-bulb,
No direct hit to smash the shatter-proof
And lodge at last the quivering needle
Clean in the eye of one who stands transfixed
In fascination of her brightness.

The Fly

O hideous little bat, the size of snot,
With polyhedral eye and shabby clothes,
To populate the stinking cat you walk
The promontory of the dead man's nose,
Climb with the fine leg of a Duncan-Phyfe
    The smoking mountains of my food
        And in a comic mood
    In mid-air take to bed a wife.

Riding and riding with your filth of hair
On gluey feet or wing, forever coy,
Hot from the compost and green sweet decay,
Sounding your buzzer like an urchin toy—
You dot all whiteness with diminutive stool,
    In the tight belly of the dead
        Burrow with hungry head
    And inlay maggots like a jewel.

At your approach the great horse stomps and paws
Bringing the hurricane of his heavy tail;
Shod in disease you dare to kiss my hand
Which sweeps against you like an angry flail;
Still you return, return, trusting your wing
    To draw you from the hunter's reach
        That learns to kill to teach
    Disorder to the tinier thing.

My peace is your disaster. For your death
Children like spiders cup their pretty hands
And wives resort to chemistry of war.
In fens of sticky paper and quicksands
You glue yourself to death. Where you are stuck
    You struggle hideously and beg,
        You amputate your leg
    Imbedded in the amber muck.

But I, a man, must swat you with my hate,
Slap you across the air and crush your flight,
Must mangle with my shoe and smear your blood,
Expose your little guts pasty and white,
Knock your head sidewise like a drunkard's hat,
    Pin your wings under like a crow's,
        Tear off your flimsy clothes
And beat you as one beats a rat.

Then like Gargantua I stride among
The corpses strewn like raisins in the dust,
The broken bodies of the narrow dead
That catch the throat with fingers of disgust.
I sweep. One gyrates like a top and falls
    And stunned, stone blind, and deaf
        Buzzes its frightful F
And dies between three cannibals.

The Leg

Among the iodoform, in twilight-sleep,
What have I lost? he first inquires,
Peers in the middle distance where a pain,
Ghost of a nurse, hazily moves, and day,
Her blinding presence pressing in his eyes
And now his ears. They are handling him
With rubber hands. He wants to get up.

One day beside flowers near his nose
He will be thinking, *When will I look at it?*
And pain, still in the middle distance, will reply,
At what? and he will know it's gone,
O where! and begin to tremble and cry.
He will begin to cry as a child cries
Whose puppy is mangled under a screaming wheel.

Later, as if deliberately, his fingers
Begin to explore the stump. He learns a shape
That is comfortable and tucked in like a sock.
This has a sense of humor, this can despise
The finest surgical limb, the dignity of limping,
The nonsense of wheel-chairs. Now he smiles to the wall:
The amputation becomes an acquisition.

For the leg is wondering where he is (all is not lost)
And surely he has a duty to the leg;
He is its injury, the leg is his orphan,
He must cultivate the mind of the leg,
Pray for the part that is missing, pray for peace
In the image of man, pray, pray for its safety,
And after a little it will die quietly.

The body, what is it, Father, but a sign
To love the force that grows us, to give back
What in Thy palm is senselessness and mud?
Knead, knead the substance of our understanding
Which must be beautiful in flesh to walk,
That if Thou take me angrily in hand
And hurl me to the shark, I shall not die!

The Progress of Faust

He was born in Deutschland, as you would suspect,
And graduated in magic from Cracow
In Fifteen Five. His portraits show a brow
Heightened by science. The eye is indirect,
As of bent light upon a crooked soul,
And that he bargained with the Prince of Shame
For pleasures intellectually foul
Is known by every court that lists his name.

His frequent disappearances are put down
To visits in the regions of the damned
And to the periodic deaths he shammed,
But, unregenerate and in Doctor's gown,
He would turn up to lecture at the fair
And do a minor miracle for a fee.
Many a life he whispered up the stair
To teach the black art of anatomy.

He was as deaf to angels as an oak
When, in the fall of Fifteen Ninety-four,
He went to London and crashed through the floor
In mock damnation of the playgoing folk.
Weekending with the scientific crowd,
He met Sir Francis Bacon and helped draft
"Colours of Good and Evil" and read aloud
An obscene sermon at which no one laughed.

He toured the Continent for a hundred years
And subsidized among the peasantry
The puppet play, his tragic history;
With a white glove he boxed the devil's ears
And with a black his own. Tired of this,
He published penny poems about his sins,
In which he placed the heavy emphasis
On the white glove which, for a penny, wins.

Some time before the hemorrhage of the Kings
Of France, he turned respectable and taught;
Quite suddenly everything that he had thought
Seemed to grow scholars' beards and angels' wings.
It was the Overthrow. On Reason's throne
He sat with the fair Phrygian on his knees
And called all universities his own,
As plausible a figure as you please.

Then back to Germany as the sages' sage
To preach comparative science to the young
Who came from every land in a great throng
And knew they heard the master of the age.
When for a secret formula he paid
The Devil another fragment of his soul,
His scholars wept, and several even prayed
That Satan would restore him to them whole.

Backwardly tolerant, Faustus was expelled
From the Third Reich in Nineteen Thirty-nine.
His exit caused the breaching of the Rhine,
Except for which the frontier might have held.
Five years unknown to enemy and friend
He hid, appearing on the sixth to pose
In an American desert at war's end
Where, at his back, a dome of atoms rose.

Tornado Warning

It is a beauteous morning but the air turns sick,
The April freshness seems to rot, a curious smell,
Above the wool-pack clouds a rumor stains the sky,
A fallow color deadening atmosphere and mind.
The air gasps horribly for breath, sucking itself
In spasms of sharp pain, light drifts away.
Women walk on grass, a few husbands come home,
Bushes and trees stop dead, children gesticulate,
Radios warn to open windows, tell where to hide.

The pocky cloud mammato-cumulus comes on,
Downward-projecting bosses of brown cloud grow
Lumps on lymphatic sky, blains, tumors, and dugs,
Heavy cloud-boils that writhe in general disease of sky,
While bits of hail clip at the crocuses and clunk
At cars and windowglass.

                      We cannot see the mouth,
We cannot see the mammoth's neck hanging from cloud,
Snout open, lumbering down ancient Nebraska
Where dinosaur lay down in deeps of clay and died,
And towering elephant fell and billion buffalo.
We cannot see the horror-movie of the funnel-cloud
Snuffing up cows, crazing the cringing villages,
Exploding homes and barns, bursting the level lakes.

Travelogue for Exiles

Look and remember. Look upon this sky;
Look deep and deep into the sea-clean air,
The unconfined, the terminus of prayer.
Speak now and speak into the hallowed dome.
What do you hear? What does the sky reply?
The heavens are taken: this is not your home.

Look and remember. Look upon this sea;
Look down and down into the tireless tide.
What of a life below, a life inside,
A tomb, a cradle in the curly foam?
The waves arise; sea-wind and sea agree
The waters are taken: this is not your home.

Look and remember. Look upon this land,
Far, far across the factories and the grass.
Surely, there, surely, they will let you pass.
Speak then and ask the forest and the loam.
What do you hear? What does the land command?
The earth is taken: this is not your home.

Troop Train

It stops the town we come through. Workers raise
Their oily arms in good salute and grin.
Kids scream as at a circus. Business men
Glance hopefully and go their measured way.
And women standing at their dumbstruck door
More slowly wave and seem to warn us back,
As if a tear blinding the course of war
Might once dissolve our iron in their sweet wish.

Fruit of the world, O clustered on ourselves
We hang as from a cornucopia
In total friendliness, with faces bunched
To spray the streets with catcalls and with leers.
A bottle smashes on the moving ties
And eyes fixed on a lady smiling pink
Stretch like a rubber-band and snap and sting
The mouth that wants the drink-of-water kiss.

And on through crummy continents and days,
Deliberate, grimy, slightly drunk we crawl,
The good-bad boys of circumstance and chance,
Whose bucket-helmets bang the empty wall
Where twist the murdered bodies of our packs
Next to the guns that only seem themselves.
And distance like a strap adjusted shrinks,
Tightens across the shoulder and holds firm.

Here is a deck of cards; out of this hand
Dealer, deal me my luck, a pair of bulls,
The right draw to a flush, the one-eyed jack.
Diamonds and hearts are red but spades are black,
And spades are spades and clubs are clovers—black.
But deal me winners, souvenirs of peace.
This stands to reason and arithmetic,
Luck also travels and not all come back.

Trains lead to ships and ships to death or trains,
And trains to death or trucks, and trucks to death,
Or trucks lead to the march, the march to death,
Or that survival which is all our hope;
And death leads back to trucks and trains and ships,
But life leads to the march, O flag! at last
The place of life found after trains and death—
Nightfall of nations brilliant after war.

ART

All tropic places smell of mold

All tropic places smell of mold. A letter from Karachi smells
of mold. A book I had in New Guinea twenty years ago
smells of mold. Cities in India smell of mold and dung.
After a while you begin to like it. The curry dishes in
the fine Bombay restaurant add the dung flavor. In the
villages dung patties plastered to the walls, the leav-
ing of the cows the only cooking fuel. The smell rubs
into the blood.

Paris in the winter smells of wood smoke and fruit. Near the
Gare St. Lazare in the freezing dusk the crowds pour
slowly down the streets in every direction. A police van
the size of a Pullman car goes at a walking pace. The
gendarme keeps jumping down from the rear like a
streetcar conductor in the old days. He is examining
identity cards of pedestrians, especially the females. A
girl comes swinging along, her pocketbook in rhythm
with her behind. She is bareheaded and wears a rain-
coat. The gendarme examines her identity card. She is
motioned into the paddy wagon.

Salzburg, the castle smells of snow and peat. Baltimore, old
oaken bucket. Portsmouth, Virginia, roses and diesel oil.
Dublin, coal dust, saccharine whiskey, bitter bodies.
Damp gusts of Siena doorways. Warehouses of Papeete,
acrid smell of copra, frangipani, salt water and mold.
Smell of rotting water in Hollandia.

Unbreathable jungles, parks subtle and cool. Backstage the
ballet dancers wipe their sweat; "the entire stage stinks
like a stable." Sewer gas of beauty parlors. Electric
smell of hair in rut. Talcum powder, earliest recollec-
tion. Rome, the armpit of the universe.

A Calder

To raise an iron tree
Is a wooden irony,
But to cause it to sail
In a clean perpetual way
Is to play
Upon the spaces of the scale.
Climbing the stairs we say,
Is it work or is it play?

Alexander Calder made it
Work and play:
Leaves that will never burn
But were fired to be born,
Twigs that are stiff with life
And bend as to the magnet's breath,
Each segment back to back,
The whole a hanging burst of flak.

Still the base metals,
Touched by autumnal paint
Fall through no autumn
But, turning, feint
In a fall beyond trees,
Where forests are not wooded,
There is no killing breeze,
And iron is blooded.

A Parliament of Poets

Two hundred poets are sitting side by side
In the government auditorium,
Waiting their turn to mount the stage
And read five minutes' worth of poems,
And then sit down again, still side by side,
The young, the old, the crazy, the sane
In alphabetical order.
Some rant their lines, some plead and some intone,
Some bellow and some simply talk.

Outside along the curb there waits a line
Of blue government buses
To carry the poets to the White House to shake hands
With the young President. The President
Is interested in shaking hands with the poets
And possibly saying something to each.

But when the alphabet has run its course
The chairman takes the lectern to announce
That the trip to the White House is called off,
The visit has been postponed
Or canceled for an indefinite period.

It appears that the President has chosen this hour
To warn the nation that a fleet of freighters,
Carrying atomic warheads on their decks
Visibly, are moving towards the coast of Cuba,
And that the President has ordered our fleet
To intercept and blockade the invaders.

And the parliament of poets disintegrates,
Some going to their hotel rooms to pack,
Some to the dark bars, some to the streets
To gaze up at the vacant Washington sky.

Connecticut Valley

Call it the richest pocket in the world,
Which rumored in the ear of Milton's breed
Once bore the freeborn Englishman across,
Or from God-ridden Massachusetts, down.

A while the Indian stinking from his paint
Stalked the white villages and counted scalps
But turned, lacking concealment, to the hills,
Or else fell, richer by a musket ball,

Leaving the land divided, as were fit,
Between the men with implements to scratch,
Rescratch and smooth and currycomb the dirt
March after March unto the present hour.

Good Yankees these, and round about the sane
Practical hearts who fashioned all the nails
For the new nation, carving in spare time
Wooden nutmegs to sell to willing fools;

Ruling themselves by blue laws, painting pure
The plain church, blending beauty with the snow.
Death for adultery in the pretty towns
And strictness in the fields for centuries.

After three hundred years the motorist
Happening by may marvel at these streets
Where every dwelling bears the building date
In homage to the beauty of great age;

Where every ghost is laid, knowing how well
The pride of house is kept, both in the fields
Where dark tobacco sweetens under gauze,
Cows calve, corn stretches to the yellow sun;

And where on lawns the Sunday gentry meet,
Insurance writers, toolmakers in tweeds,
The fibrous sons and daughters of the state
Driving hard bargains through the afternoon.

Garage Sale

Two ladies sit in the spotless driveway
Casually smoking at the not-for-sale card table,
Over their heads a row of plastic pennants,
Orange, yellow, assorted reds and blues,
Such as flap over used-car lots, a symbol.
Each thing for sale is hand-marked with a label,
And every object shows its homemade bruise.

They sit there all day, sometimes getting up
When a visitor asks a question about a crib
Or a box spring with a broken rib
Or a gas jet to start fireplace fires.

Cars park gently, some with daisy decals,
No Mark IV's, Coupe de Villes or Corvettes;
Mostly wagons with the most copious interiors,
And few if any intellectuals.

All day the shoppers in low-key intensities,
Hoping to find something they are trying to remember
Fits in, or sticks out, approach and mosey,
Buy a coffee mug with a motto, or leave,
And nobody introduces him or herself by name.
That is taboo. And nobody walks fast. That is taboo.
And those who come look more or less the same.

A child buys a baby dress for her Raggedy Ann.
A pair of andirons, a mono hi-fi, a portable
                typewriter, square electric fan,
Things obsolescing but not mature enough to be
                antiques,
And of course paintings which were once expensive
Go or can go for a song.

This situation, this neighborly implosion,
As flat as the wallpaper of Matisse
Strikes one as a cultural masterpiece.
In this scene nothing serious can go wrong.

Haircut

O wonderful nonsense of lotions of Lucky Tiger,
Of savory soaps and oils of bottle-bright green,
The gold of liqueurs, the unguents of Newark and Niger,
Powders and balms and waters washing me clean;

In mirrors of marble and silver I see forever
Increasing, decreasing the puzzles of luminous spaces,
As I turn, am revolved and am pumped in the air on a lever,
With the backs of my heads in chorus with all of my faces.

Scissors and comb are mowing my hair into neatness,
Now pruning my ears, now smoothing my neck like a plain;
In the harvest of hair and the chaff of powdery sweetness
My snow-covered slopes grow dark with the wooly rain.

And the little boy cries, for it hurts to sever the curl,
And we too are quietly bleating to part with our coat.
Does the barber want blood in a dish? I am weak as a girl,
I desire my pendants, the fatherly chin of a goat.

I desire the pants of a bear, the nap of a monkey
Which trousers of friction have blighted down to my skin.
I am bare as a tusk, as jacketed up as a flunkey,
With the chest of a moth-eaten camel growing within.

But in death we shall flourish, you summer-dark leaves of my
    head,
While the flesh of the jaw ebbs away from the shores of my
    teeth;
You shall cover my sockets and soften the boards of my bed
And lie on the flat of my temples as proud as a wreath.

Impact

High up on the patio window, centered exactly,
suddenly I see in a certain light
the ghost of a bird, like a memorial,
as finely etched as a fossil,
outline of a bird
where it smacked the window hard,
the glass a perfect replica of sky,
thinking it was sky,
the sky that struck it down.

The wings are printed separately,
delicately pointed at either end
like two hummingbirds standing in flight
aimed at each other, past an invisible head
— there is no head —
but the neck is written
and a few body-feathers splayed like tiny fans
and even the legs a parenthesis
and two black blood spots plain as periods.

So that's what it was the child bent over
that the cat was eating,
leaving high up on the patio window
the negative of a bird,
mirage born of a mirage.

The wind has all but washed the feathers away.
The cat is licking its beautiful arrogant leg.

Manhole Covers

The beauty of manhole covers—what of that?
Like medals struck by a great savage khan,
Like Mayan calendar stones, unliftable, indecipherable,
Not like the old electrum, chased and scored,
Mottoed and sculptured to a turn,
But notched and whelked and pocked and smashed
With the great company names
(Gentle Bethlehem, smiling United States).
This rustproof artifact of my street,
Long after roads are melted away will lie
Sidewise in the grave of the iron-old world,
Bitten at the edges,
Strong with its cryptic American,
Its dated beauty.

New Museum

Entering the new museum we feel first
The rubbery values of a doctor's walls,
Cinnamon, buff, gunmetal, rose of gray,
But these almost immediately fade away,
Leaving the windowless white light
That settles only on the works of art—
A far cry from the stained cathedrals where
Masterpieces crack in the bad air
Of candle grease, conversation, and prayer
Ours is the perfect viewing atmosphere.

Walking around, we are much quieter here
Than in the great basilicas,
The great basilicas of Christendom.
Those freezing niches were the masters' home;
Our galleries warm us like a hotel room
Of cinnamon, powder blue, eggshell of rose,
And yet our painters paint as from a bruise,
The blues neither transparent nor opaque,
The blacks so dry they seem a dust of black.
These are the patterns which our feelings make.

They paint their images as if through smoke,
With now and then a falling coal of red
And now and then a yellow burst, like shock;
They paint the damaged tissue magnified,
The lower land, the structure of the thing;
They paint the darkened luminous optic lake
Through which our eyes, though blind,
See all the lines of force and points of stress
In the scientific field of dark.
These are the patterns which our feelings make.

There is such light in darkness that we see
Blueprints of dreams, child's play, prehistory,
And caves and Altamiras of the mind;
These painters kiss with open eyes to make

Miles of Picassos and the double nose.
Soothed by the blues and blacks, our eyes unclose
To drink great gulps of darkness in;
O skies that fall away time after time
Where tracers of emotion miss the mark
But leave the patterns which our feelings make!

These images have all come home like crows
That cross the hot wheat of the last van Goghs
And cross everything out;
His sorrow saw the thick-skinned peeling sun
Explode above the terrified sunflowers.
Our painters stumble through his private night,
Follow the weak shout of the electric light
Deeper into the caves and offices
Where doctors hang abstractions, blue and black.
These are the patterns which our feelings make.

Photographs of the Poets On Looking into a Recent Anthology

As if the inner voice had said, *Don't smile*,
Not one is smiling, as photographers prefer,
But each poet has his chin up, so to speak,
And each poet is in profile, as it were.
The compositions on the whole are weak
And yet suggest the formal Brady style.

Poets are good-looking. It's hard to say just why.
The mouths are poor, often the lips are fat,
The hair of an obvious or a dated cut.
It's difficult to point to this or that
Feature—the ears, for instance—and say what
Precisely makes the pictures catch the eye.

In little ovals and cropped squares they pose,
The sensual, the ethereal, and the vain,
And jut their graceful jawbones into view.
Sometimes the cheeks show deeper grooves of pain
Than in most faces. Nevertheless it's true
The really telltale organ is the nose.

The poet's nose is like a bird in flight;
The winged nostrils buff the shining wind.
The poet's nose is like a speeding prow
That splits the silk of waves and leaves behind
The widening incision of the bow;
The poet's nose is like a bull-tongue plow.

But lesser men have noble noses, too.
It is the look that makes the poet's face;
The look of inside-out, the look of wax,
Of wizened innocence and the skinless gaze;
It is the staring mask that never cracks
Or, when it does, splits dangerously through.

Aged and beardless boys with doubled fists
And girls, old girls, in sibylline disguise,
What is it that the popping camera asks
The flickering silence of your rows of eyes?
What light can penetrate your ancient masks
Or the bright glow of your myopic mists?

Poet

Il arrive que l'esprit demande la poesie

Left leg flung out, head cocked to the right,
Tweed coat or army uniform, with book,
Beautiful eyes, who is this walking down?
Who, glancing at the pane of glass looks sharp
And thinks it is not he—as when a poet
Comes swiftly on some half-forgotten poem
And loosely holds the page, steady of mind,
        Thinking it is not his?

And when will *you* exist?—Oh, it is I,
Incredibly skinny, stooped, and neat as pie,
Ignorant as dirt, erotic as an ape,
Dreamy as puberty—with dirty hair!
Into the room like kangaroo he bounds,
Ears flopping like the most expensive hound's;
His chin receives all questions as he bows
        Mouthing a green bon-bon.

Has no more memory than rubber. Stands
Waist-deep in heavy mud of thought and broods
At his own wetness. When he would get out,
To his surprise he lifts in air a phrase
As whole and clean and silvery as a fish
Which jumps and dangles on his damned hooked grin,
But like a name-card on a man's label
        Calls him a conscious fool.

And child-like he remembers all his life
And cannily constructs it, fact by fact,
As boys paste postage stamps in careful books,
Denoting pence and legends and profiles,
Nothing more valuable.—And like a thief,
His eyes glassed over and congealed with guilt,
Fondles his secrets like a case of tools,
        And waits in empty doors.

By men despised for knowing what he is,
And by himself. But he exists for women.
As dolls to girls, as perfect wives to men,
So he to women. And to himself a thing,
All ages, epicene, without a trade.
To girls and wives always alive and fated;
To men and scholars always dead like Greek
        And always mistranslated.

Towards exile and towards shame he lures himself,
Tongue winding on his arm, and thinks like Eve
By biting apple will become most wise.
Sentio ergo sum: he feels his way
And words themselves stand up for him like Braille
And punch and perforate his parchment ear.
All language falls like Chinese on his soul,
        Image of song unsounded.

This is the coward's coward that in his dreams
Sees shapes of pain grow tall. Awake at night
He peers at sounds and stumbles at a breeze.
And none holds life less dear. For as a youth
Who by some accident observes his love
Naked and in some natural ugly act,
He turns with loathing and with flaming hands,
        Seared and betrayed by sight.

He is the business man, on beauty trades,
Dealer in arts and thoughts who, like the Jew,
Shall rise from slums and hated dialects
A tower of bitterness. Shall be always strange,
Hunted and then sought after. Shall be sat
Like an ambassador from another race
At tables rich with music. He shall eat flowers,
Chew honey and spit out gall. They shall all smile
        And love and pity him.

His death shall be by drowning. In that hour
When the last bubble of pure heaven's air

Hovers within his throat, safe on his bed,
A small eternal figurehead in terror,
He shall cry out and clutch his days of straw
Before the blackest wave. Lastly, his tomb
Shall list and founder in the troughs of grass
                And none shall speak his name.

Poet in Residence

for Stuart Wright

To some it's a jewel in the belt of Alma Mater,
To others Beware of the Dog,
To some it's a jetstream from heaven,
To others an acid rain.
    The poet shy and bold as a bullet
    Arrives at his residence
    Booted and spurred but often with tie.
To some that man is patently impossible,
To others potentiality in person.
    The Muse is standing at the open door,
    The poet takes her in his arms.
    Here are the books, she says, here are the beds.
To some he is a danger to the republic,
To others the cause thereof.
    At the window he asks the names of the trees,
    At the window she weeps with open relief.
To some he muddies the conjugation of numbers,
To others he is the decimal.
    She leads him to the extremities of the map,
    To the shores of the immemorial
    For the sake of his residence.
To some he is lost to society forever,
To others society is lost without him.
    The carillons ring in the campus towers at dusk,
    The bats do squareroot over the ivory tower.

Randall, I like your poetry terribly

Randall, I like your poetry terribly, yet I'm afraid to say so. Not that my praise keeps you awake—though I'm afraid it does. I can't help liking them. I even like the whine, the make-believe whiplash with the actual wire in it. Once when you reviewed me badly (you must) I wrote you: "I felt as if I had been run over but not hurt." That made you laugh. I was happy. It wasn't much of a triumph but it worked. When people ask about you I am inclined to say: He's an assassin (a word I never use). I'm inclined to say: Why are you always yourself? Your love of Rilke—if it's love—your intimacy with German and God knows what all, your tenderness and terrorization, your prose sentences—like Bernini graves, staggeringly expensive, Italianate, warm, sentences once-and-for-all. And the verses you leave half-finished in mid-air—I once knew a woman who never finished a sentence. Your mind is always at its best, your craft the finest craft "money can buy" you would say with a barb. I'm afraid of you. Who wouldn't be. But I rush to read you, whatever you print. That's news.

The bourgeois poet

The bourgeois poet closes the door of his study and lights his
pipe. Why am I in this box, he says to himself (although
it is exactly as he planned). The bourgeois poet sits down
at his inoffensive desk—a door with legs, a door turned
table—and almost approves the careful disarray of books,
papers, magazines and such artifacts as thumbtacks. The
bourgeois poet is already out of matches and gets up.
It is too early in the morning for any definite emotion
and the B.P. smokes. It is beautiful in the midlands:
green fields and tawny fields, sorghum the color of red
morocco bindings, distant new neighborhoods, cleanly
and treeless, and the Veterans Hospital fronted with a
shimmering Indian Summer tree. The Beep feels sea-
sonal, placid as a melon, neat as a child's football lying
under the tree, waiting for whose hands to pick it up.

The Humanities Building

All the bad Bauhaus comes to a head
In this gray slab, this domino, this plinth
Standing among the olives or the old oak trees,
As the case may be, and whatever the clime.
No bells, no murals, no gargoyles,
But rearing like a fort with slits of eyes
Suspicious in the aggregate, its tons
Of concrete, glaciers of no known color,
Gaze down upon us. Saint Thomas More,
Behold the Humanities Building!
                                    On the top floor
Are one and a half professors of Greek,
Kicked upstairs but with the better view,
And two philosophers, and assorted Slavics;
Then stacks of languages coming down,
Mainly the mother tongue and its dissident children
(History has a building all its own)
To the bottom level with its secretaries,
Advisors, blue-green photographic light
Of many precious copying machines
Which only the girls are allowed to operate.
And all is bathed in the cool fluorescence
From top to bottom, justly distributed
Light, Innovation, Progress, Equity;
Though in my cell I hope and pray
Not to be confronted by
A student with a gun or a nervous breakdown,
Or a girl who closes the door as she comes in.

The Old Guard sits in judgment and wears ties,
Eying the New in proletarian drag,
Where the Assistant with one lowered eyelid
Plots against Tenure, dreaming of getting it;

And in the lobby, under the bulletin boards,
The Baudelairean forest of posters

For Transcendental Meditation, Audubon Group,
"The Hunchback of Notre Dame," Scientology,
Arab Students Co-op, "Case of the Curious Bride,"
Two students munch upon a single sandwich.

The Intellectual

What should the wars do with these jigging fools?

The man behind the book may not be man,
His own man or the book's or yet the time's,
But still be whole, deciding what he can
In praise of politics or German rimes;

But the intellectual lights a cigarette
And offers it lit to the lady, whose odd smile
Is the merest hyphen—lest he should forget
What he has been resuming all the while.

He talks to overhear, she to withdraw
To some interior feminine fireside
Where the back arches, beauty puts forth a paw
Like a black puma stretching in velvet pride,

Making him think of cats, a stray of which
Some days sets up a howling in his brain,
Pure interference such as this neat bitch
Seems to create from listening disdain.

But talk is all the value, the release,
Talk is the very fillip of an act,
The frame and subject of the masterpiece
Under whose film of age the face is cracked.

His own forehead glows like expensive wood,
But back of it the mind is disengaged,
Self-sealing clock recording bad and good
At constant temperature, intact, unaged.

But strange, his body is an open house
Inviting every passerby to stay;
The city to and fro beneath his brows
Wanders and drinks and chats from night to day.

Think of a private thought, indecent room
Where one might kiss his daughter before bed!
Life is embarrassed; shut the family tomb,
Console your neighbor for his recent dead;

Do something! die in Spain or paint a green
Gouache, go into business (Rimbaud did),
Or start another Little Magazine,
Or move in with a woman, have a kid.

Invulnerable, impossible, immune,
Do what you will, your will will not be done
But dissipate the light of afternoon
Till evening flickers like the midnight sun,

And midnight shouts and dies: I'd rather be
A milkman walking in his sleep at dawn
Bearing fat quarts of cream, and so be free,
Crossing alone and cold from lawn to lawn.

I'd rather be a barber and cut hair
Than walk with you in gilt museum halls,
You and the puma-lady, she so rare
Exhaling her silk soul upon the walls.

Go take yourselves apart, but let me be
The fault you find with everyman. I spit,
I laugh, I fight; and you, *l'homme qui rît*,
Swallow your stale saliva, and still sit.

The living rooms of my neighbors

The living rooms of my neighbors are like beauty parlors, like night-club powder rooms, like international airport first-class lounges. The bathrooms of my neighbors are like love nests—Dufy prints, black Kleenex, furry towels, toilets so highly bred they fill and fall without a sigh (why is there no bidet in so-clean America?). The kitchens of my neighbors are like cars: what gleaming dials, what toothy enamels, engines that click and purr, idling the hours away. The basements of my neighbors are like kitchens; you could eat off the floor. Look at the furnace, spotless as a breakfront, standing alone, prize piece, the god of the household.

But I am no different. I arrange my books with a view to their appearance. Some highbrow titles are prominently displayed. The desk in my study is carefully littered; after some thought I hang a diploma on the wall, only to take it down again. I sit at the window where I can be seen. What do my neighbors think of me—I hope they think of me. I fix the light to hit the books. I lean some rows one way, some rows another.

A man's house is his stage. Others walk on to play their bit parts. Now and again a soliloquy, a birth, an adultery.

The bars of my neighbors are various, ranging from none at all to the nearly professional, leather stools, automatic coolers, a naked painting, a spittoon for show.

The businessman, the air-force captain, the professor with tenure—it's a neighborhood with a sky.

The Pigeons

In the denouement of the beautiful storm
A pair of pigeons landed on the ledge
With barely a purchase for their feet,
The female and her mate.
There was no sill
Eleven stories above the street.
They seemed to peer at two small pigeons
Carved of glass, one blue, one green
On the inside, only an inch away.

Is that why they were here
Or were they blown by chance, these doves,
Into a momentary conjunction
By some maker's dream?

The Poetry Reading

He takes the lectern in his hands
And, like a pilot at his instruments,
Checks the position of his books, the time,
The glass of water, and the slant of light;
Then, leaning forward on guy-wire nerves,
He elevates the angle of his nose
And powers his soul into the evening.

Now, if ever, he must begin to climb
To that established height
Where one hypnotically remains aloft,
But at the thought, as if an engine coughed,
He drops, barely clearing the first three rows,
Then quakes, recovers, and upward swerves,
And hangs there on his perilous turning fans.

O for more altitude, to spin a cloud
Of crystals, as the cloud writes poetry
In nature's wintry sport!
Or for that hundred-engined voice of wings
That, rising with a turtle in its claws,
Speeds to a rock and drops it heavily,
Where it bursts open with a loud report!

O for that parchment voice of wrinkled vowels,
That voice of all the ages, polyglot,
Sailing death's boat
Past fallen towers of foreign tours—
The shrouded voice troubled with stony texts,
Voice of all souls and of sacred owls,
Darkly intoning from the tailored coat!

Or for the voice of order, witty and good,
Civilizing the ears of the young and rude,
Weaving the music of ideas and forms,
Writing encyclopedias of hope.
Or for that ever higher voice that swarms

Like a bright monkey up religion's rope
To all those vacant thrones.

But he who reads thinks as he drones his song:
What do they think, those furrows of faces,
Of a poet of the middle classes?
Is he a poet at all? His face is fat.
Can the anthologies have his birthday wrong?
He looks more like an aging bureaucrat
Or a haberdasher than a poet of eminence.

He looks more like a Poet-in-Residence

O to be *declassé*, or low, or high,
Criminal, bastard, or aristocrat—
Anything but the norm, the in-between!
Oh, martyr him for his particular vice,
Make him conspicuous at any price,
Save him, O God, from being nice.

Whom the gods love die young. Too late for that,
Too late also to find a different job,
He is condemned to fly from room to room
And, like a parakeet, be beautiful,
Or, like a grasshopper in a grammar school,
Leap for the window that he'll never find,
And take off with a throb and come down blind.

The Sawdust Logs

for Bill Everson

When wood went up and the price of fire soared
Sky-high, we bought some sawdust logs.
In a waxed box, lumpen, they lay,
Poor waxen stumps, perfectly round,
Lifeless and cool, with a nostalgic sawdust smell.
A lover of oak and almond and eucalyptus
I felt a little ashamed. Another substitute.
Well, why shouldn't sawdust have its day?

They do exactly as they say,
Separate into slices, inch-thick wheels,
Or hang together like a magnum lobster,
Blackening but not reddening in the fire,
Pale fire, voiceless, colorless
Except for a gaseous yellow ghost,
Odorless, wintry, hardly conducive
To salamandrine dream or spicy phoenix.
One tends not to look at it at all.
The eye would rather settle on TV.

Where are the gunshots, the fire fountains?

An honest fake electric fire with a shadow fan
Would be better than this.
Or a lifelike log of steel with neat gas flowers,
Which you go up to and can't believe exists.

At least they're not those other Sterno logs,
Poison green, technicolor blue, that advertise their B.T.U.'s,
Making you think of gas masks,
Château-Thierry, Newark, New Jersey.
This at least is what it is, poor ghost.

And in the morning, ash of sawdust log
Lies hardly visible, dust mice, cigaret ash,
With a welfare smell,
Or perhaps, like crematorium ash,
Too mortal and too fine,
All but a trace, joyless, eternal,
Consumed, consumed, consumed.

They held a celebration for you, Charles

They held a celebration for you, Charles, in Iowa. I was asked
but I regretted. It was the hundredth birthday of your
book, your proper Christian book called *Flowers of
Evil*. (Or is it THE *Flowers of Evil*? I never know.)
And in that hymnal, how well you made yourself in
the image of Poe—Poe with a cross, that's what you
are, adored of the gangster age. In fact, aren't you a
children's poet? Aren't you the Lewis Carrol of small
vice? Your shabby Wonderland of pus and giant nipple,
your cats and jewels and cheap perfumes, your licking
Lesbians and make-believe Black Mass, O purulence of
Original Sin. And always playing it safe in the end,
like Disneyland. So many safety devices, pulleys, cranks,
classical alexandrines. It's Iowa for you, restless spirit,
where elderly ladies embezzle millions in the *acte
gratuite*. You'll need no naturalization papers here. And
yet I loved you once, and Delacroix and Berlioz—all in
my gangster age. The little boy in me loved you all, O
solemn Charles, so photogenic. And this is my flower
for your anniversary. I fashioned it of Mexican tin and
black nail polish, little French Swinburne burning in
Iowa City.

University

To hurt the Negro and avoid the Jew
Is the curriculum. In mid-September
The entering boys, identified by hats,
Wander in a maze of mannered brick
    Where boxwood and magnolia brood
    And columns with imperious stance
    Like rows of ante-bellum girls
        Eye them, outlanders.

In whited cells, on lawns equipped for peace,
Under the arch, and lofty banister,
Equals shake hands, unequals blankly pass;
The exemplary weather whispers, "Quiet, quiet"
    And visitors on tiptoe leave
    For the raw North, the unfinished West,
    As the young, detecting an advantage,
        Practice a face.

Where, on their separate hill, the colleges,
Like manor houses of an older law,
Gaze down embankments on a land in fee,
The Deans, dry spinsters over family plate,
    Ring out the English name like coin,
    Humor the snob and lure the lout.
    Within the precincts of this world
        Poise is a club.

But on the neighboring range, misty and high,
The past is absolute: some luckless race
Dull with inbreeding and conformity
Wears out its heart, and comes barefoot and bad
    For charity or jail. The scholar
    Sanctions their obsolete disease;
    The gentleman revolts with shame
        At his ancestor.

And the true nobleman, once a democrat,
Sleeps on his private mountain. He was one
Whose thought was shapely and whose dream was broad;
This school he held his art and epitaph.
    But now it takes from him his name,
    Falls open like a dishonest look,
    And shows us, rotted and endowed,
        Its senile pleasure.

What kind of notation is in my *Time* file

What kind of notation is in my *Time* file for my life, especially
     my death? Will they say I died, O God? If they don't
     say I died how can I die? There it is fine and relevant
     to die, an honor so to speak, interesting as divorce.

What's in my file at the F.B.I.? What's my symbol when they
     flick me out? Am I a good American or a borderline
     case? Can I hold my liquor? Have I ever been cleared,
     and if so, of what?

Dear Fame, I meet you in the damnedest places. You smile,
     you walleyed bitch, but you look over my shoulder for
     a prearranged signal: something has come up on the
     other side of the room.

My life, my own, who is writing you on what pale punch
     cards? Deep-thinking machine, have you got my num-
     ber?

A hundred oligarchs in identical suits are sitting around a table
     shaped like a uterus, alphabetizing greatness. I say to
     myself: all men are great. I would like to cry but have
     forgotten how. Now I remember: they used to come
     to me, those journalists with humble pencils. They
     begged me from their hats: say something big; give us
     an execution; make bad weather. I failed them badly.
     I couldn't grow a beard.

I guess I haven't built my ship of death. The word "image" is
     now in government. The doors are all closing by re-
     mote control. But when I meet the almighty Publicity
     Director, name-dropper of kings, I'll shake his hand
     and say: once I kissed Fame (mouth like an ass hole)
     but only for fun. He'll tear up the punch cards and
     think for a minute.

GOD

A Modest Funeral

Death passed by on fervid rubber wheels.
Three broad mortuary Cadillacs,
Flying modest pennants low on the fenders,
Led the procession, followed by a covey
Of medium-priced cars, with no overcrowding,
And some with just a driver at the wheel,
But the whole cluster with headlights lit,
As is the law and custom of the thoroughfare.

Only at the rear was there any sign of jostling,
Any suggestion of impatient thought
At foolish delay; or *Where's the funeral!*

Death passed at moderate speed and slowed the counter-traffic
To a respectful twenty, making it almost veer,
As when one hears a siren in the distance.

Then it was gone, the funeral with its flags
And fine sparkling lights, like tears in the eyes,
Gone to the silvered fences at the edge of town,
And the soft gravel of the cemetery.

I am an atheist who says his prayers

I am an atheist who says his prayers.

I am an anarchist, and a full professor at that. I take the loyalty
  oath.

I am a deviate. I fondle and contribute, backscuttle and brown,
  father of three.

I stand high in the community. My name is in *Who's Who*.
  People argue about my modesty.

I drink my share and yours and never have enough. I free-load
  officially and unofficially.

A physical coward, I take on all intellectuals, established poets,
  popes, rabbis, chiefs of staff.

I am a mystic. I will take an oath that I have seen the Virgin.
  Under the dry pandanus, to the scratching of kangaroo
  rats, I achieve psychic onanism. My tree of nerves elec-
  trocutes itself.

I uphold the image of America and force my luck. I write my
  own ticket to oblivion.

I am of the race wrecked by success. The audience brings me
  news of my death. I write out of boredom, despise
  solemnity. The wrong reason is good enough for me.

I am of the race of the prematurely desperate. In poverty of
  comfort I lay gunpowder plots. I lapse my insurance.

I am the Babbitt metal of the future. I never read more than
  half of a book. But that half I read forever.

I love the palimpsest, statues without heads, fertility dolls of
  the continent of Mu. I dream prehistory, the invention

of dye. The palms of the dancers' hands are vermillion. Their heads oscillate like the cobra. High-caste woman smelling of earth and silk, you can dry my feet with your hair.

I take my place beside the Philistine and unfold my napkin. This afternoon I defend the Marines. I goggle at long cars.

Without compassion I attack the insane. Give them the horse-whip!

The homosexual lectures me brilliantly in the beer booth. I can feel my muscles soften. He smiles at my terror.

Pitchpots flicker in the lemon groves. I gave down on the plains of Hollywood. My fine tan and my arrogance, my gray hair and my sneakers, O Israel!

Wherever I am I become. The power of entry is with me. In the doctor's office a patient, calm and humiliated. In the foreign movies a native, shabby enough. In the art gallery a person of authority (there's a secret way of approaching a picture. Others move off). The high official insults me to my face. I say nothing and accept the job. He offers me whiskey.

How beautifully I fake! I convince myself with men's room jokes and epigrams. I paint myself into a corner and escape on pulleys of the unknown. Whatever I think at the moment is true. Turn me around in my tracks; I will take your side.

For the rest, I improvise and am not spiteful and water the plants on the cocktail table.

*   *   *

When I dismissed you, friend, why did I do that? The Judas in me is strong. With an effort I regain my loyalty,

and lose it again. These virtues incapacitate me. The
solitude of the masochist is mine.

Albatross of a prize, you who married me to a newspaper, you
who made me a government, why can't I thank you?

Kindness of deep hostility, my patience of a saint, endless capacity
for love—mother, did I have the breast really? (But
you gave me girls in your own likeness.)

This laissez-aller, this Traumdeutung—am I really a poet? Do
I give a damn? That too I betray. I cross my fingers
and exclude bedfellow death. I rub the icebox with my
swimming thighs. I embrace the white rhinoceros; I
propose to toilets.

What right have I to be healthy? What right have I to escape?
And what is it I have escaped? I explore opportunities.
(The rising sun sits on my other head. My cancer is
blooming.)

I insist on the middle-aged poet. Brats of the drunken boat,
centurions in the pay of Congress, gray and forgetful,
purposefully stupid—God bless you, and Congress.

Marvelously recapitulating man, the child, reviving literature,
invents religion. The dog flops on the floor with grace-
ful disgust.

Goldfish, I loved you. When you died I cried. I'm no biologist.
I did my best. I know. I overfed you. I was warned on
the box. (The air-force officer has a tropical tank. His
fishes glitter like a jewelry store.)

*   *   *

New York, my love, we never went to bed. (You never asked
me.) New York, my Jewess, you read me Kierkegaard
on the subway, standing up. I didn't give you a chance
to kill me, N.Y.

Chicago, what did I do to you? What's another stab in the back, Chicago?

New York, killer of poets, do you remember the day you passed me through your lower intestine? The troop train paused under Grand Central. That line of women in mink coats handed us doughnuts through the smutty windows. They were all crying. For that I forgive New York. (We smuggled a postcard off at New Haven.)

Chicago, smothered in boredom and pigs: your Gothic universities, your Portuguese wines, your bad baseball.

New York, island of prisons. New York of a billion black Rimbauds. Chicago of dreamy cardinals.

What was it like, New York, when the skyscrapers were white? New York of Hart Crane. Harlem of Lorca.

Chicago of T.S. Eliot (his city). Chicago of bad impulses.

$$*\qquad*\qquad*$$

All things remain to be simplified. I find I must break free of the poetry trap.

The books I hunger for are always out, never to be returned; illuminations, personal bibles, diatribes, chapters denied acceptance in scripture, Tobit blinded by sparrows muting warm dung in his eyes, immense declarations of revolt, manuals of the practice of love.

I seek the entrance of the rabbit hole. Maybe it's the door that has no name.

My century, take savagery to your heart. Take wooden idols, walk them through the streets. Bow down to Science.

My century that boils history to a pulp for newspaper, my century
of the million-dollar portrait, century of the decipher-
ment of Linear B and the old scrolls, century of the
dream of penultimate man (he wanders among the aban-
doned skyscrapers of Kansas; he has already forgotten
language), century of the turning-point of time, the
human wolf pack and the killing light.

*   *   *

Crazy-clean, our armies and bodies. Crazy-clean the institutions
of the mind. Crazy-clean Washington, D.C.

The generals say: mop up, no sweat, cordon sanitaire, liquidate,
flush, wipe out.
How many have escaped the prison of Art? Who has not been
extradited? Through the blue grid of technique we read
the wild faces.

Stanza means room, with bars on it. Form means shape, beaten
and maimed. It is done, ingeniously done, immortally done.
For a century or two it pleases and instructs.

Now and again, one of the slaves escapes. His eyes are put out
with platinum hatpins.

To escape to America. How is it there? Do the bluecoats smile?

The little ones file into the classroom. The giggling dies down.
They salute the flag. They bow their heads. Childhood
is over. When the air raid sounds they crouch on the
floor like Moslems. It's only for practice of course.

I tell the secret of the starving artist. A day after he died the
chauffeurs knocked at the door.

Poets of early death, who overturned the boat? Physician John
Keats, cure thyself!

Lists of the mad and bibles of the damned. Dictionaries of suicide, card indexes of the compulsive revolutionaries, Protestant cemeteries of sacred remains. Beatification of the Dutchman's ear. Under the dome of poetry an array of saints as broken as christological glass. Martyrology of prosodists. Mariolatary of Hebrews. Every twilight of the mind for sale.

Counterfeiters, defenders of hell-gate. The intentionally mad, aristocrats of the verb, apologists of exile, culture nationalists, founders of the Next Phase.

Studies of the decrease of light. Paintings of right angles. Poems with square edges. Literary quarterlies refined from steel.

*   *   *

The teacher recites her lesson: the poem lifts me; it tips my arrows. No matter the horror; it washes us, the blood-washed poem.

The teacher recites her lesson: this is reality; this is the ideal. This is the touch of God. My Muse, my mother, my fertile one. (A slow leak in the footnotes: the goddess bleeds apace.)

Why do you paint your lips? Is it time to eat?

The tigress rolls its cubs. The dainty sparrow, proletarian bird, lights on the horse turd, a golden bun. The mouse in the trap has exquisite fur. I touch it with my fingers before I lift it from the drawer on its well-made mouse-trap. The vertebra of the rattlesnake lies in the palm of my hand, a masterpiece of subtle bone. Where did you get it? The doll pouts: the child is learning a picture. You have to be taught to *read* a picture. The savage looks at the photograph of himself; he turns it sideways and upside-down. Why doesn't it register?

127

The class convenes in the library attic. I introduce myself and
throw their books out of the window. We will write a
poem together, I say. (I see the gothic in their eyes.)
It turns out nicely.

My Utamaro is pea green. I see what Vincent saw.

Sunday cut into colored squares, *Chicago Tribune*, Japanese
print of future generations, I collect your yellows and
washy blues. Bold line of Dick Tracy, Lautrec of mur-
der, sexless, decisive, one riddle solved, a fresh body
produced. Your palindromes, a villain named Etah.
Evil, said Carroll, is live spelled backwards.

Permanent orphan of generations, has daddy gone to fight the
Communists with his private army and his diamond stick-
pin? Carrot-top orphan who still says *Hark!*

Cornbeef and cabbage man, pining for the brownstone days.
Matronly Maggie with a rolling pin. (Pogo and Pea-
nuts leave me cold.)

Sirens with black lips and identical faces. Fly-boys in the Orient;
regulation uniforms.

Tillie and Mack in the Kinsey Collection. In New Guinea the
Japanese propaganda drawings dropped from a Zero:
Yank, this is what civilian is doing to your wife back
home. (Showing what.) Colors of Utamaro.

Frank Merriwell at Yale. Tom the fun-loving Rover. Tom
Swift and his electric grandmother (joke). Alger, Henty,
S. S. Van Dine.

"Patterns" by Amy Lowell. And in Virginia, *Southern Prose
and Poetry*.

Books for the sake of shelves. Encyclopedia of railroad engi-
neering, sixty-seven volumes, fold-out plates of boilers,

piston assembly. The Waverly novels, dark tomes maroon and brown to handle on a rainy day. Balzac complete, unread. *The Harvard Classics*, mean, unprovocative, *Veritas* stamped on the backbone.

* * *

Poem, is it de rigueur to descend to hell? Will you lose your pedigree?

How businesslike is convention. What slag the prodigies of the epic mind. How little human the heroes and angels.

Tell me again what tragedy is. I can never remember.

Because the king is a fool and the lady a bitch; because a woman butchers her children to spite her husband; or a man makes love to his mother by mistake—shall I descend to hell?

Because the dollar tips the scales; or certain languages are dead; the nobility bankrupt; because the government has awarded you teeth—shall I descend to hell?

I descend and find the usual evidence. And Paul made love to Frances and they burn forever.

Where are you taking me, Alighieri? I have a different religion. I go with Geoffrey to the house of April. Gottfried of Strassburg, give us the gutsy Tristan.

Children play on the gorgeous baldaquin, climbing the marble vines while the mothers kneel, eating the Body. The priest moves rapidly from mouth to mouth. Black and white, the barbaric tower rears over history. It's no playground.

The bloodshot Germans enter the Forum in shorts. Proudly they gaze on the fine destruction.

In Bombay the vegetarians storm the hotel: "You are eating the flesh of the god!" A dirty cow stands in the doorway of the office building. A Hindu gives it a kick in the rump and sends it off in the rain.

I teach the emotions. The head is hugeness already. Sin is ruled out. A tropic laugh splits heaven up the middle.

The disciplinarians stalk between the flowers. The whips crash on the bitten fingernails. It's war from the start. The books are weighted with lead. The catechism demands more algebra. Down on your knees.

Who teaches manners of fear? Who teaches reverence of wealth? Why so many books? What fabulous detail, what attractive bindings! Did you take the Intelligence Test this morning? Would you like to learn Russian?

The mind, the mind, cleaned like a car, purring like a fan. And the feelings matted and stuck, scratching the lice of love.

Do you hate your face? It is your sex you hate. Worship has pigged your eyes.

*   *   *

O love, phenomenon of attention, hear me out! I hold the shaving mirror to all:

To you at breakfast with folded newspaper,

You with the telephone in your hand and the glass name on the door,

You the alumnus, recipient of telegraphed congratulation,

You on election night, you in the driver's seat,

You in dutiful coitus, you in social drunkenness, you in parental storm;

At the cornerstone, near the triumphal arch, on the cruise deck,
in the ad for bitters,

In the photograph of the first lieutenant, signed, "Ages ago,"

In the vestry room with the males and the white flower,

In the waiting room of the daffodil maternity ward,

At the elegant tent beside the open grave (the coffin glows like
a fine piano);

To you saluting, you baring your head, you holding the scissor
to the early rose—

Did you know the damasked walls give way so rottenly, the
gilded wood so mealy with fatigue?

Did you see the estates divided and plowed and the monstrous
houses opened to view for your sad Sundays?

Aren't you the popular song of God in the formstone churches,
you of ideals and virtues, responsible, lovable, disciplined,
free?

Isn't it you you mutter against, with your fuzzed haircut in
your wife's bosom?

Citizen, is your glorious revolution over and done with?

And you, my country, how does it feel to be They?

What are those objects on which our eyes are frozen?

Flag on the candy-factory grammar school;

Eternal light hung from a silver chain above the Ark in the
synagogue;

Samurai sword in the French admiral's possession (to be given to a poet on a state occasion);

Rectilinear façade of Greek; font of the Hebrew; spittle of the christer contorting on the bare ground;

Finder of inscapes; critique of frameless abstractions; voyeurs of myth;

Hypnotized lovers; Napoleonic captains of copper mines; editors of quack compendia of knowledge;

All worshipers, all fanatics, all absorbed in the object which is really you,

You who descry the streamings of life as other and beyond;

You strapped to your muscles (is the culture-gag in your teeth?);

Altars, uniforms of every description, detritus of battles, delirium of ethics, codes of the good, new wars, new medals, new masterpieces forged for the market;

Heavy stone of your overturned lives, what crawling dreams!

What is it you are trying to become, men of my species?

Homo normalis, blind as a bat, that music you hear is coming from you. Where did you study the physics of the epic? What is this eternal conspiracy of distraction? Why are the sick the most articulate? Poetry weaving at the bar, go home. Somebody call a cab.

Who are these that compound the mystery? Tell me about the Dewey Decimal System.

Do something about the sour smell of schools. Call the Americans!

Herewith I abolish up and down. Future and past for those with radial vision.

Everything everywhere has been decided in everyone's favor.

I end on the dead level and peter out. Is it time for the curtain?
Shall we applaud at the end of the second movement?

*   *   *

I love Nowhere where the factories die of malnutrition.

I love Nowhere where there are no roads, no rivers, no in-
teresting Indians,

Where history is invented in the History Department and there
are no centennials of anything,

Where every tree is planted by hand and has a private tutor,

Where the "parts" have to be ordered and the sky settles all
questions,

Where travelers from California bitch at the backwardness and
New Yorkers step on the gas in a panic,

Where the grass in winter is gray not brown,

Where the population diminishes.

Here on the boundary of the hired West, equidistant from every
tourist office, and the air is washed by distance, here at
last there is nothing to recommend.

May no one ever attempt a recommendation; Chicago be as far
as Karachi.

Though the warriors come with rockets, may they fall off the
trucks.

May the voting be light and the clouds like a cruise and the
criminal boredom enter the district of hogs.

I love Nowhere where the human brag is a brag of neither time nor place,

But an elephant house of Smithsonian bones and the white cathedrals of grain,

The feeding-lots in the snow with the steers huddled in symmetrical misery, backs to the sleet,

To beef us up in the Beef State plains, something to look at.

*   *   *

To the poor (aux pauvres) crime alone (le crime seul) opens (ouvre) les portes de la vie (the doors of life). Entire libraries of music are hurled in the gutters: the G.I.'s are looking for bottles. The Bavarian Venus is snatched baldheaded.

I have a big sister; she has mighty breasts. She writes poems for the immigration office. Her crotch is on the fourteenth floor. La géante, la géante!

Standing at the pure white rail, stately we pass you, and the classes mingle as if by degree. At the last buoy the discreet signs begin to take effect: First Class, Second Class. My brazen sister swirling her nightgown, green as the spouts of Chartres. Her comb is combing my lice (but I have no lice). Her apron is hitched up in front. She stands on a full-sized bank.

Across the iambic pentameter of the Atlantic (the pilot dropped, the station wagon in the hold) we sail to the kingdom of Small. Is it cheaper there? Can I buy a slave?

This is the camera with the built-in lie. This is the lens that defies the truth. There's nothing for it but to write the large bad poem in middle-class magic. Poem condemned to wear black, be quoted in churches, versatile as Greek. Condemned to remain unsung by criminals.

In India

In India, the people form among the trees
With a rubbery quiet; on farthest roads
Surround you with a rubbery tread.
I stand in their circles of wonder like a light
Shining in eyes grown vague with centuries
Of stunned obedience and heartbreaking loads,
Not tall, I tower above them by a head;
Pale, I pass through their never-ending night.

A crow came to my window by the sea
At four o'clock in the Taj Mahal Hotel;
He cocked his eye and when I turned my back
Flew to my tea tray with a hideous clack
Of beak and claws, turning over the tea
And making off with the cake. The crow did well,
For down below me, where the street was black
With white-clad Hindus, what was there to take?

And foreigners say the poverty is the cause,
Thinking that gold can cure the old disease,
Thinking that oil can make the old wheel turn.
I see a new landmark on the long skyline,
An edifice of seamless stone and glass
Topped by the great word *Standard* in the skies.
Toward the Arabian Sea I watch it burn
And, being American, feel that it is mine!

And still the native voices, soft as sand,
Cry, "Master! Master!" as a professional saint
Might roll his eyes and faint into his god
In the middle of traffic. Still thy call aloud
"Sahib, Master!" and hold out their hand.
And lovely women with a moon of paint
Daubed on their foreheads shake hands and fade
Into silence, bowing with a praying bow.

These beautiful, small millions turn to stone
Before your eyes, become soft sculpture swarming up
The slant of temples, where their thighs protrude
Half out of joint, the angles of their arms
Twist in voluptuous torsion, and their bones
Fold into symbols pliable as rope.
The walls are sluggish with their multitude
Of gods and dancers and half-human forms.

But are they gods or droppings of the gods?
Is this the mire in which they all submerge,
This bog of holiness which ingurgitates
Prophet and hero, turning them to stone?
Which are the deities, which the human clods?
Or in this jungle do they truly merge?
And where is Reason in this hive of faith—
The one god missing from this pantheon?

I see a new god carved in fresh relief,
The brown saint in the shining spectacles
Who took the hand of the untouchables,
Who wove all India from a skein of thread.
Now he and all their spinning wheels are gone,
For a young Hindu, under whose homespun
Lay a revolver, knelt and, in good faith,
Received his blessing and then shot him dead.

Israel

When I think of the liberation of Palestine,
When my eye conceives the great black English line
Spanning the world news of two thousand years,
My heart leaps forward like a hungry dog,
My heart is thrown back on its tangled chain,
My soul is hangdog in a Western chair.

When I think of the battle for Zion I hear
The drop of chains, the starting forth of feet
And I remain chained in a Western chair.
My blood beats like a bird against a wall,
I feel the weight of prisons on my skull
Falling away; my forebears stare through stone.

When I see the name of Israel high in print
The fences crumble in my flesh; I sink
Deep in a Western chair and rest my soul.
I look the stranger clear to the blue depths
Of his unclouded eye. I say my name
Aloud for the first time unconsciously.

Speak of the tillage of a million heads
No more. Speak of the evil myth no more
Of one who harried Jesus on his way
Saying, *Go faster*. Speak no more
Of the yellow badge, *secta nefaria*.
Speak the name only of the living land.

Messias

Alone in the darkling apartment the boy
Was reading poetry when the doorbell rang;
The sound sped to his ear and winged his joy,
The book leaped from his lap on broken wing.

Down the gilt stairwell then he peered
Where an old man of patriarchal race
Climbed in an eastern language with his beard
A black halo around his paper face.

His glasses spun with vision and his hat
Was thick with fur in the August afternoon;
His silk suit crackled heavily with light
And in his hand a rattling canister shone.

Bigger he grew and softer the root words
Of the hieratic language of his heart,
And faced the boy, who flung the entrance wide
And fled in terror from the nameless hurt.

Past every door like a dead thing he swam,
Past the entablatures of the kitchen walls,
Down the red ringing of the fire escape
Singing with sun, to the green grass he came,

Sickeningly green, leaving the man to lurch
Bewildered through the house and seat himself
In the sacrificial kitchen after his march,
To study the strange boxes on the shelf.

There mother found him mountainous and alone,
Mumbling some singsong in a monotone,
Crumbling breadcrumbs in his scholar's hand
That wanted a donation for the Holy Land.

Necropolis

Even in death they prosper; even in the death
Where lust lies senseless and pride fallow
The mouldering owners of rents and labor
Prosper and improve the high hill.

For theirs is the stone whose name is deepest cut,
Theirs the facsimile temple, theirs
The iron acanthus and the hackneyed Latin,
The boxwood rows and all the birds.

And even in death the poor are thickly herded
In intimate congestion under streets and alleys.
Look at the standard sculpture, the cheap
Synonymous slabs, the machined crosses.

Yes, even in death the cities are unplanned.
The heirs govern from the old centers;
They will not remove. And the ludicrous angels,
Remains of the poor, will never fly
But only multiply in the green grass.

The Alphabet

The letters of the Jews as strict as flames
Or little terrible flowers lean
Stubbornly upwards through the perfect ages,
Singing through solid stone the sacred names.
The letters of the Jews are black and clean
And lie in chain-line over Christian pages.
The chosen letters bristle like barbed wire
That hedge the flesh of man,
Twisting and tightening the book that warns.
These words, this burning bush, this flickering pyre
Unsacrifices the bled son of man
Yet plaits his crown of thorns.

Where go the tipsy idols of the Roman
Past synagogues of patient time,
Where go the sisters of the Gothic rose,
Where go the blue eyes of the Polish women
Past the almost natural crime,
Past the still speaking embers of ghettos,
There rise the tinder flowers of the Jews.
The letters of the Jews are dancing knives
That carve the heart of darkness seven ways.
These are the letters that all men refuse
And will refuse until the king arrives
And will refuse until the death of time
And all is rolled back in the book of days.

The Cathedral Bells

luxury liners laden with souls

All day the yellow elevator cage
Rises and falls in the scaffolding
Clutching the biggest cathedral in the world
Like a yellow bee on a climb to a flower
That hasn't opened yet.
The yellow elevator moves at a crawl
To a tower still on the drawing-board.

In morning when I open my eyes I see
The massive cathedral with topless towers
And my heart leaps up, though I'm no christian;
I understand the vocational clamber of bees,
The tired endeavor, not quite in good faith
Since the rich have moved away.

Incredible in this megalopolis of sheerest skyscrapers
To be wakened in the morning by cathedral bells,
Deep bells competing with sixteen-wheeler rigs,
Anger of cop-cars, bleat of ambulances,
Coughing of towering-inferno ladder-trucks.

Returned by such tintinabulations
One half expects to hear a rooster crow
Or a soft drum-roll of rain
Or the slapping of branches, as the giant bells
Outsound even the thrumming of jetplanes

And the pulmonary windmills of helicopters
As the timekeepers of God
Goldenly, leadenly beat out the hours
With a wistful Doppler effect,
And no bell towers visible anywhere,
All very tired, not quite in good faith
Since the rich have moved away.

The priest so far away looks like a speck
Under a nave as tall as the *Queen Mary*.
Such immensity must be called-for!
In a minor corner a man is praying in Spanish,
A thousand candles finger the expensive gloom
As in a firstclass dining saloon
Of infinite tables set with silver and lace.
Are we in steerage or in first class?

The entire island sways like a ship,
Slanting its funnels, upping its prow to the moon.
Are we sinking or breaking a transatlantic record?
There seems to be some kind of accord,
A couple of seagulls cruise across the scene
At surveillance height, looking for god knows what,
Blown by the wind, between two rivers.
The speck of a priest tinkles his tiny bell,
Awakening an appetite for wine
In the cathedral of St. John the Divine,
All very tired, not quite in good faith
Since the rich have moved away.

The Crucifix in the Filing Cabinet

Out of the filing cabinet of true steel
That saves from fire my rags of letters, bills,
Manuscripts, contracts, all the trash of praise
Which one acquires to prove and prove his days;

Out of the drawer that rolls on hidden wheels
I drew a crucifix with beaded chain,
Still new and frightened-looking and absurd.
I picked it up as one picks up a bird

And placed it on my palm. It formed a pile
Like a small mound of stones on which there stands
A tree crazy with age, and on the tree
Some ancient teacher hanging by his hands.

I found a velvet bag sewn by the Jews
For holy shawls and frontlets and soft thongs
That bind the arm at morning for great wrongs
Done in a Pharoah's time. The crucifix

I dropped down in the darkness of this pouch,
Thought tangled with thought and chain with chain,
Till time untie the dark with greedy look,
Crumble the cross and bleed the leathery vein.

The Dirty Word

The dirty word hops in the cage of the mind like the Pondi-cherry vulture, stomping with its heavy left claw on the sweet meat of the brain and tearing it with its vicious beak, ripping and chopping the flesh. Terrified, the small boy bears the big bird of the dirty word into the house, and grunting, puffing, carries it up the stairs to his own room in the skull. Bits of black feather cling to his clothes and his hair as he locks the staring creature in the dark closet.

All day the small boy returns to the closet to examine and feed the bird, to caress and kick the bird, that now snaps and flaps its wings savagely whenever the door is opened. How the boy trembles and delights at the sight of the white excrement of the bird! How the bird leaps and rushes against the walls of the skull, trying to escape from the zoo of the vocabulary! How wildly snaps the sweet meat of the brain in its rage.

And the bird outlives the man, being freed at the man's death-funeral by a word from the rabbi.

But I one morning went upstairs and opened the door and entered the closet and found in the cage of my mind the great bird dead. Softly I wept it and softly removed it and softly buried the body of the bird in the hollyhock garden of the house I lived in twenty years before. And out of the worn black feathers of the wing have I made pens to write these elegies, for I have outlived the bird, and I have murdered it in my early manhood.

The Interlude

I

Much of transfiguration that we hear,
The ballet of the atoms, the second law
Of thermo-dynamics, Isis, and the queer

Fertilization of fish, the Catholic's awe
For the life-cycle of the Nazarene,
His wife whom sleeping Milton thought he saw;

Much of the resurrection that we've seen
And taken part in, like the Passion Play,
All of autumnal red and April green,

To those who walk in work from day to day,
To economic and responsible man,
All, all is substance. Life that lets him stay

Uses his substance kindly while she can
But drops him lifeless after his one span.

II

What lives? the proper creatures in their homes?
A weed? the white and giddy butterfly?
Bacteria? necklaces of chromosomes?

What lives? the breathing bell of the clear sky?
The crazed bull of the sea? Andean crags?
Armies that plunge into themselves to die?

People? A sacred relic wrapped in rags,
The ham-bone of a saint, the winter rose,
Do these?—And is there not a hand that drags

The bottom of the universe for those
Who still perhaps are breathing? Listen well,
There lives a quiet like a cathedral close

At the soul's center where substance cannot dwell
And life flowers like music from a bell.

III
Writing, I crushed an insect with my nail
And thought nothing at all. A bit of wing
Caught my eye then, a gossamer so frail

And exquisite, I saw in it a thing
That scorned the grossness of the thing I wrote.
It hung upon my finger like a sting.

A leg I noticed next, fine as a mote,
"And on this frail eyelash he walked," I said,
"And climbed and walked like any mountain-goat."

And in this mood I sought the little head,
But it was lost; then in my heart a fear
Cried out, "A life—why beautiful, why dead!"

It was a mite that held itself most dear,
So small I could have drowned it with a tear.

The password of the twentieth century

The password of the twentieth century: Communications (as
if we had to invent them). Animals and cannibals have
communications; birds and bees and even a few human
creatures, called artists (generally held to be insane).
But the bulk of humanity had to invent Communica-
tions. The Romans had the best roads in the world, but
had nothing to communicate over them except other
Romans. Americans have conquered world-time and
world-space and chat with the four corners of the earth
at breakfast and have nothing to communicate except
other Americans. The Russians communicate other Rus-
sians to the moon. The entire solar system is in the hands
of cartoonists.

I am sitting in the kitchen in Nebraska and watching a shrouded
woman amble down the market in Karachi. She is going
to get her morning smallpox shot. It's cold and mental
love they want: It's the mystic sexuality of Communi-
cations. Money was love. Power was love. Communi-
cations now are love. Sex-object of the telephone, let's
kiss. The girl hugs the hi-fi speaker to her belly: it pours
into her openings like gravy. In the spring, Hitler arises.
This is the time of trampling. My japanned birds in the
radioactive snow are calling.

A man appears at the corner of the street; I prepare myself for
hospitality. Man or angel, welcome! But I am afraid
and double-lock the door. On the occasion of the death
of a political party, I send an epitaph by Western Union.
I didn't go to the funeral of poetry. I stayed home and
watched it on television. Moon in the bottom of the
Steuben glass, sun nesting in New Mexican deserts—the
primitive Christian communicated with a dirty big toe.
He drew a fish in the dust.

The Synagogue

The synagogue dispirits the deep street,
Shadows the face of the pedestrian,
It is the adumbration of the Wall,
The stone survival that laments itself,
Our old entelechy of stubborn God,
Our calendar that marks a separate race.

The swift cathedral palpitates the blood,
The soul moves upward like a wing to meet
The pinnacles of saints. There flocks of thanks
In nooks of holy tracery arrive
And rested take their message in mid-air
Sphere after sphere into the papal heaven.

The altar of the Hebrews is a house,
No relic but a place, Sinai itself,
Not holy ground but factual holiness
Wherein the living god is resident.
Our scrolls are volumes of the thundered law
Sabbath by sabbath wound by hand to read.

He knows Al-Eloah to whom the Arab
Barefooted falls on sands, on table roofs,
In latticed alleys underneath the egg
On wide mosaics, when the crier shrills.
O profitable curse, most sacred rug,
Your book is blindness and your sword is rust.

And Judenhetze is the course of time;
We were rebellious, all but Abraham,
And skulked like Jonah, angry at the gourd.
Our days are captives in the minds of kings,
We stand in tens disjointed on the world
Grieving the ribbon of a coast we hated.

Some choose the ethics of belief beyond
Even particular election. Some

In bland memorial churches modify
The architecture of the state, and heaven
Disfranchised watches, caput mortuum,
The human substance eating, voting, smiling.

The Jew has no bedecked magnificat
But sits in stricken ashes after death,
Refusing grace; his grave is flowerless,
He gutters in the tallow of his name.
At Rome the multiplying tapers sing
Life endless in the history of art.

And Zion womanless refuses grace
To the first woman as to Magdalene,
But half-remembers Judith or Rahab,
The shrewd good heart of Esther honors still,
And weeps for almost sacred Ruth, but doubts
Either full harlotry or the faultless birth.

Our wine is wine, our bread is harvest bread
That feeds the body and is not the body.
Our blessing is to wine but not the blood
Nor to sangreal the sacred dish. We bless
The whiteness of the dish and bless the water
And are not anthropaphagous to him.

The immanent son then came as one of us
And stood against the ark. We have no prophets,
Our scholars are afraid. There have been friars,
Great healers, poets. The stars were terrible.
At the Sadducee court he touched our panic;
We were betrayed to sacrifice this man.

We live by virtue of philosophy,
Past love, and have our devious reward.
For faith he gave us land and took the land,
Thinking us exiles of all humankind.
Our name is yet the identity of God
That storms the falling altar of the world.

The Tingling Back

Sometimes deeply immured in white-washed tower
    quiet at ink and thinking book,
        alone with my own smoke,
the blood at rest, the body far below,
    swiftly there falls an angry shower
        of arrows upon my back,
like bees or electric needles run amok
    between my flesh and shirt. I know
        then I have touched the pain
of amour-propre, of something yesterday
    I said and I should not have said,
        I did and must not do.
These needles wing their insights from my brain
    and through and through my flesh they play
        to prick my skin with red
letters of shame and blue blurs of tattoo.
    I sweat and take my medicine
        for one must be sincere
and study one's sincerity like a crime:
    to be the very last to smile,
        the first one to begin
(when danger streaks the atmosphere) to fear,
    to pocket praises like a dime,
        to pet the crocodile,
to see a foreign agony as stone,
    to ravel dreams in crowded room,
        to let the hair grow tall,
to skin the eye and thrust it to the wind.
    Yet if I stood with God alone
        inside the blinding tomb
I would not feel embarrassment at all
    nor those hot needles of the mind
        which are so clean. I'd ask
not if I'd known the tissue of my will
    and scarified my body white,
        but whether, insincere,
I'd grown to the simplicity of a mask;

and if in natural error still
whether my fingers might
destroy the true and keep the error near.

Washington Cathedral

From summer and the wheel-shaped city
That sweats like a swamp and wrangles on
Its melting streets, white mammoth Forums,
And political hotels with awnings, caryatids;
Past barricaded embassies with trees
That shed trash and parch his eyes,
To here, the acres of superior quiet,
Shadow and damp, the tourist comes,
And, cooled by stones and darkness, stares.

Tall as a lover's night, the nave
Broods over him, irradiates,
And stars of color out of painted glass
Shoot downward on apostles and on chairs
Huddled by hundreds under altar rails.
Yet it is only Thursday; there are no prayers,

But exclamations. The lady invokes by name
The thousand-odd small sculptures, spooks,
New angels, pitted roods; she gives
The inventory of relics to his heart
That aches with history and astonishment:
He gives a large coin to a wooden coffer.

Outside, noon blazes in his face like guns.
He goes down by the Bishop's walk, the dial,
The expensive grass, the Byzantine bench,
While stark behind him a red naked crane
Hangs over the unfinished transept,
A Cubist hen rivalling the Gothic School.

Whether he sees the joke; whether he cares;
Whether he tempts a vulgar miracle,
Some deus ex machina, this is his choice,
A shrine of whispers and tricky penumbras.
Therefore he votes again for the paid

Clergy, the English hint, the bones of Wilson
Crushed under tons of fake magnificence.
      Nor from the zoo of his instincts
      Come better than crude eagles: now
He cannot doubt that violent obelisk
And Lincoln whittled to a fool's colossus.
This church and city triumph in his eyes.
He is only a good alien, nominally happy.